favorite recipes from

Melissa Clark's Kitchen

favorite recipes from

Melissa Clark's Kitchen

Family Meals, Festive Gatherings,
and everything in-between

Melissa Clark

PHOTOGRAPHS BY DANA GALLAGHER

BLACK DOG
& LEVENTHAL
PUBLISHERS
NEW YORK

Black Dog & Leventhal Publishers
Hachette Book Group
1290 Avenue of the Americas
New York, NY 10104
www.hachettebookgroup.com
www.blackdogandleventhal.com

First Edition: April 2018

Black Dog & Leventhal Publishers is an imprint of Hachette Books, a division of
Hachette Book Group. The Black Dog & Leventhal Publishers name and logo
are trademarks of Hachette Book Group, Inc.
The publisher is not responsible for websites (or their content) that are not owned by the publisher.

Print book interior design by Alison Lew, Vertigo Design NYC

Library of Congress Control Number: 2017951929
ISBNs: 978-0-316-35414-1 (hardcover); 978-0-316-35415-8 (ebook)

Printed in China
1010
10 9 8 7 6 5 4 3 2 1

contents

introduction

A question that I often get asked is, out of the thousands of recipes I've developed for my cookbooks and column over the years, which ones are my absolute favorites? This seems like a pretty straightforward query to the person asking it. But for me, it can be puzzling. How can I whittle down decades of work into just a handful of dishes that I can quickly list off? Because the truth of it is, every dish has its time and place. Before I can start mentally scanning all the chicken dishes in my roster to recommend one (or ten), I need to understand how and when said dish would be served. Give me the context, and the ideas start flowing like an ice-cold Rye Manhattan into a chilled cocktail coupe (with Spiced Nuts on the side, please).

Are we talking favorite after-work meals? Farro Pasta with Spicy Salami Tomato Sauce will fit the bill for families with big kids, Roasted Chicken Thighs with Apples for families with little ones. And for the kid-less—or on kid-less nights when summer camp or sleepovers have absorbed your children—Buttery, Garlicky, Spicy Calamari couldn't be easier or more delicious. Or perhaps you're eating alone, cozy on the couch in front of your favorite movie. A big bowl of Carroty Mac and Cheese (to supply the vegetable quotient) isn't just for families, but for anyone in need of something creamy, comforting, and supremely satisfying but quick to make.

If it's fancy dinner party fare in question, for starters, do I suggest Port-Glazed Stilton with Homemade Oat Biscuits, or Crispy Onion Fritters? Depends on if you're a make-it-ahead or last-minute-type cook, because both are recurring favorites at dinner parties *chez moi*. Then maybe I'd follow it up with tender, rich Braised Leg of Lamb and some Israeli couscous on the side, and a lovely crisp spinach salad. Or if you aren't as in love with lamb as I am, I'd suggest my Braised Pork Shoulder with Tomatoes, Cinnamon, and Olives. And for dessert, is it summer when you've got fresh plums waiting to be turned into an Upside-Down Plum Polenta Cake? Or winter, when a Triple Chocolate Trifle is more fitting to the blustery time of year?

In this volume, I've collected enough of my favorite recipes to provide answers for every inquirer. No matter the occasion, no matter the season, no matter your craving, you're sure to find something here to make for dinner—or lunch, or even a special breakfast when you're dying for a Spanish potato tortilla instead of the usual fried eggs.

To help you prepare for any culinary circumstances that come your way, every recipe is tagged as a Weekday Staple, Perfect for Two, Family Meal, or Company's Coming. The occasion charts on pages viii–xi will help you both create menus and provide quick ideas when you need them.

Of course, these recipes are not restricted to these categories alone. Perfect for Two can still be very kid-friendly, for example, and you can add extra side dishes or double recipes as needed for more people. Weekday Staples can be great for company; in fact, casual entertaining on a school night is underrated. And so on.

All these recipes have been published before in two of my other books: *In the Kitchen with a Good Appetite* and *Cook This Now*. But here, I've chosen my personal favorites to put in one volume. Even better, these recipes are illustrated with new photos, allowing you to see many more of the dishes than you could before.

I hope the recipe collection and the photos inspire you to find your own favorites. And then when someone asks what you love to cook for company, or for your kids, or for a late-night snack, you'll know exactly what to say.

weekday staples

perfect for two

occasion charts

family meals

company's coming

occasion charts

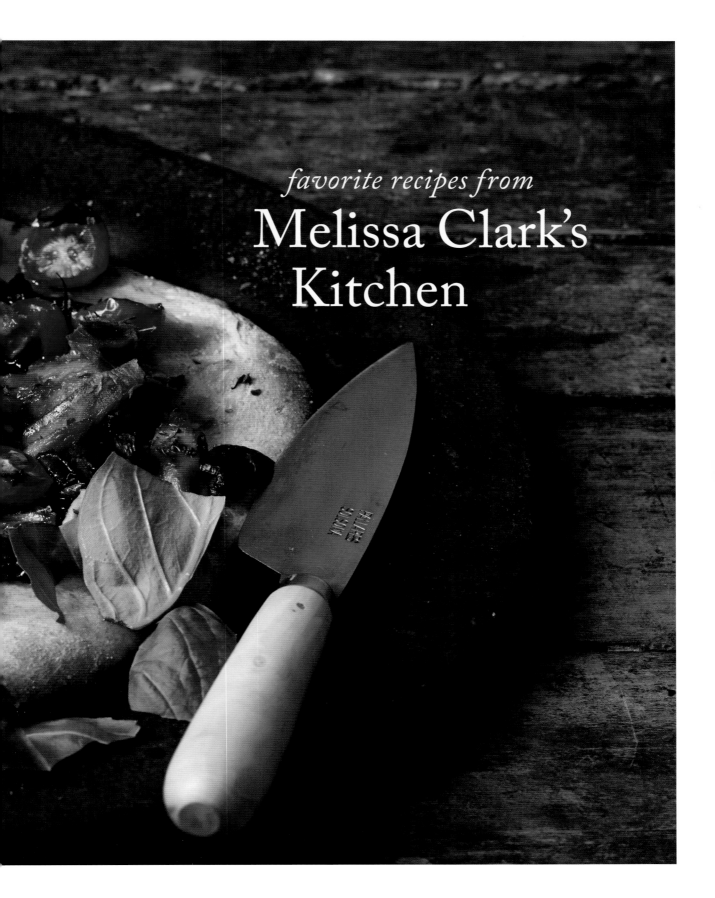

favorite recipes from
Melissa Clark's
Kitchen

breakfast/
brunch

Buckwheat pancakes with sliced peaches and cardamom cream syrup

I've been experimenting with a range of different whole-grain flours, and have found that I absolutely adore the complex, winey nuttiness of buckwheat flour. It's traditionally used in blinis, but since I don't make blinis very often (because I don't serve caviar very often, sadly), I decided to try it in a regular old pancake, the kind I make for breakfast on the weekends. Since I don't bother using yeast, the flavor isn't as complex as a blini, but the buttermilk gives it a nice fresh tang and the honey lends a little sweetness that makes these pancakes wonderful on their own, should you choose to forgo any syrupy distractions.

If you are interested in syrup, however, please try this oddball, creamy, exotic-scented, and utterly divine cardamom cream syrup at least once. I can't really tell you how I came up with it other than to say I like the combination of cardamom with juicy ripe peaches. And I like cardamom cream cakes, which I ate on a brief trip to Sweden. Come to think of it, they grow buckwheat in Sweden, and I'm sure my subconscious was aware of this as I made breakfast that day. So there you have it: Cardamom, cream, peaches, and buckwheat are a natural—okay, a *plausible*—combination.

In any case, it all works and tastes delicious, no matter how you connect the dots.

makes about 10 pancakes

FOR THE CARDAMOM CREAM SYRUP

1 tablespoon cardamom pods, crushed

⅓ cup sugar

¼ cup heavy cream

Pinch kosher salt

FOR THE PANCAKES

¾ cup all-purpose flour

½ cup buckwheat flour

½ cup whole wheat flour

2 teaspoons baking powder

1 teaspoon baking soda

½ teaspoon kosher salt

1 large egg, lightly beaten

1 tablespoon honey

2 cups buttermilk, plain yogurt, or sour cream (or a combination), plus more as needed

3 tablespoons unsalted butter, melted, plus more as needed

Sliced fresh peaches, for serving

1. MAKE THE SYRUP: In a small saucepan over medium high heat, combine the cardamom, sugar, and ⅓ cup water. Bring to a simmer and cook until the sugar has fully dissolved, about 5 minutes. Stir in the cream and salt and let it bubble gently for 2 minutes. Let the syrup cool completely; strain.

2. MAKE THE PANCAKES: In a large bowl, whisk together the flours, baking powder, baking soda, and salt. In a separate bowl, whisk together the egg and honey; whisk in the buttermilk and melted butter. Form a well in the dry ingredients. Pour the wet ingredients into the well and stir until just combined.

3. Melt some butter on a griddle or in a large skillet over medium-high heat. Working in batches, spoon ¼-cup dollops of the batter onto the griddle. Cook the pancakes until bubbles form on the surface and the edges begin to set, 2 to 3 minutes. Flip and cook until golden, 1 to 2 minutes more. Cook the remaining batter, adding more butter to the skillet between batches if necessary. Serve the pancakes hot, topped with the cardamom syrup and peaches.

The mysterious David Dares pancake

As I was growing up, my mother made what she called her "David Dares" pancake. I loved that pancake, with its airy, souffléd custard that browned in the oven, and its glazed-sugar top drizzled with a zippy burst of lemon. My mother baked it in a gratin dish deep enough for the eggs to set into a wiggly, flanlike layer beneath the buoyant, crunchy crust that deflated dramatically when you dug in.

The original recipe came from a story in the *New York Times*; the pancake was named after David Eyre, a gentleman in Hawaii with whom food editor Craig Claiborne once had brunch. Mr. Eyre got the recipe from a cookbook published in 1919, which recommended serving the pancake for dessert.

Naturally, when I made his original recipe, I could not suppress the urge to tweak. I added a little salt to deepen the flavor, and an extra egg to mimic the thick, flanlike quality of my mother's version. Call it a German pancake, a Dutch baby, or clafouti, a puffy baked pancake is a basic foodstuff common to cultures with surfeits of milk and eggs, or at least a taste for sweet, custardy things. In my family, we didn't want to wait until after dinner, so we did, and still do, eat our "David Dares" pancakes for breakfast.

serves 4

3 large eggs, lightly beaten

½ cup milk

½ cup all-purpose flour

¼ teaspoon freshly grated nutmeg

Pinch kosher salt

4 tablespoons (½ stick) unsalted butter

2 tablespoons confectioners' sugar

2 tablespoons freshly squeezed lemon juice (from about ½ lemon)

1. Preheat the oven to 425°F.

2. In a medium bowl, whisk together the eggs, milk, flour, nutmeg, and salt until combined. The mixture will still have some lumps.

3. In a 10-inch ovenproof skillet over medium heat, melt the butter. Carefully pour in the pancake batter and transfer the skillet to the oven. Bake until the pancake is puffy and golden brown around the edges, about 15 minutes.

4. Working quickly, take the skillet out of the oven and, using a fine-mesh sieve, shake the confectioners' sugar over the pancake. Return the skillet to the oven until the butter has been absorbed into the pancake and the sugar is lightly caramelized, an additional 2 to 3 minutes.

5. Splash the lemon juice over the pancake, cut into wedges, and serve immediately.

Buttery polenta with Parmesan and olive oil–fried eggs and Swiss chard

Given the American predilection for cold cereal, it's odd that hot cereal beyond oatmeal less frequently enters the picture. But grits and her first cousin on the Italian side, polenta—served soft and steaming, with plenty of salt, pepper, and grated cheese, paired with sautéed Swiss chard with loads of garlic and a jolt of red pepper flakes—is exactly what to have for breakfast or brunch when you're hungry for something more filling and savory than Wheaties.

Coarsely ground polenta and cornmeal are essentially the same thing, both made from ground dried corn. And they are similar to, but not exactly the same as, hominy grits, made from corn treated with an alkaline solution, a process called nixtamalization. Look for stone-ground and avoid "instant," a euphemism for pasty. Though recipes tell you to patiently stand over the pot, dutifully stirring to prevent the cornmeal from clumping up in protest, I've found a brisk whisking every couple of minutes will correct any lumpy inclinations. (Stand back between stirrings to avoid getting burned by eruptions of molten polenta.)

While the polenta is bubbling, prep and cook the Swiss chard.

As a final garnish, there's olive oil–fried eggs. Cooked sunny-side up, the runny egg yolk coats the greens and cornmeal mush like a golden, velvety sauce. It picks up and carries the flavors of the cheese, garlic, and pepper, imbuing each tender mouthful. If you cook the eggs over high heat, letting the whites get brown and crisp around the edges, they'll shatter when you bite, adding crunch to the sea of softness. It's the crowning *pièce de résistance*.

Buttery polenta with Parmesan and olive oil–fried eggs

serves 4

4½ cups water or low-sodium chicken broth or vegetable broth

1½ cups polenta (not quick cooking), coarse cornmeal, or corn grits

¾ teaspoon fine sea salt

2 to 4 tablespoons unsalted butter

¼ teaspoon freshly ground black pepper, plus more as needed

1 (1-ounce) chunk Parmesan cheese, or ¼ cup grated Parmesan cheese

2 tablespoons extra-virgin olive oil

8 large eggs

Coarse sea salt, for garnish

(continued)

1. In a large pot, bring the water or broth to a simmer. Stir in the polenta and fine sea salt. Simmer the polenta, stirring frequently but not constantly, until thickened to taste, 10 to 20 minutes. Stir in the butter and pepper and cover the pot to keep warm.

2. Using a vegetable peeler, slice the cheese chunk into slivers. (Or grate the cheese on the largest holes of a box grater.)

3. In a large skillet over medium heat, heat 1 tablespoon of the olive oil until very hot. Fry 4 of the eggs until the edges are crispy but the yolks are still runny. Transfer to a plate and repeat with the remaining oil and eggs.

4. Pile the polenta into bowls; top with the cheese and then the fried eggs. Garnish with coarse sea salt and more pepper, and serve.

Garlicky Swiss chard

serves 4

2 bunches Swiss chard, stems removed

1 tablespoon olive oil

2 garlic cloves, minced

Large pinch crushed red pepper flakes

Fine sea salt, for serving

1. Stack the chard leaves on top of one another (you can make several piles) and slice them into ¼-inch-wide strips.

2. In a very large skillet (or a soup pot) over high heat, heat the oil. Add the garlic and red pepper flakes and sauté for 30 seconds, until the garlic is fragrant. Stir in the chard, coating it in the oil. Cover the pan and cook for about 2 minutes, until wilted. Stir and cook, uncovered, for 2 minutes more. Season with salt. Serve in the same bowl as the polenta, if desired.

Green-poached eggs with spinach and chives

I call this creation "green eggs no ham," and it's an ideal vegetarian dish. Spiked with lemon zest, chives, chile, and cream, it really doesn't want bacon or ham or all the other meaty things I automatically think of when I think of eggs.

It's based on a recipe for sorrel-poached eggs that I came up with when I used to have a sorrel plant on my deck. The poor plant succumbed to the squirrels, who used it to bury (and aggressively dig up) nuts. Although I can certainly buy sorrel at the farmers' market, it's not dependably available.

Spinach, however, is always there, except in the broiling heat of summer. From September to June, I can count on finding bunches of the crinkly, dark green leaves, ready to be tossed into salads or wilted in a pan of butter or olive oil, and sometimes crowned with runny eggs.

If you do find sorrel, simply substitute it for the spinach. It will break down into more of a sauce than the spinach does, and the color will fade from verdant to olive drab, but the flavor will pop. Leave out the lemon zest if using sorrel; you won't need it.

Either way, while I like this for supper (not dinner; eggs are for supper), it's especially excellent for brunch.

serves 4

2 tablespoons unsalted butter

3 fat scallions, sliced, white and light greens kept separate from dark greens

1 garlic clove, finely chopped

⅓ cup finely chopped fresh chives

10 ounces fresh baby spinach (about 3 quarts)

¼ teaspoon kosher salt, plus more to taste

Freshly ground black pepper, to taste

⅓ cup heavy cream

Finely grated zest of 1 lemon

4 large eggs

Urfa, Aleppo, or crushed red pepper flakes (see Note, page 96), for serving

Flaky sea salt, for serving

Buttered toast, for serving

1. In a large skillet over medium-high heat, melt the butter and cook until the foam subsides. Add the white and light green portions of the scallions and the garlic and cook, stirring, until fragrant, about 30 seconds. Stir in the chives. Toss in the

(continued)

spinach, a handful at a time, letting each batch wilt slightly before adding more. Add the kosher salt and black pepper to taste. Stir in the cream and lemon zest; simmer until the spinach is very soft, about 3 minutes.

2. Using the back of a spoon, make four little indentations in the spinach—think of them as nests for the eggs. Crack the eggs into the nests. Reduce the heat to medium-low and sprinkle the eggs with kosher salt and black pepper. Cover the pan and let the eggs cook until almost opaque, about 3 minutes. Turn off the heat and let the eggs rest, covered, until done to your liking, 30 seconds for yolks that are runny (the whites should be completely cooked through), or longer if you like harder eggs.

3. Carefully scoop the eggs and greens into four bowls. Season each bowl with red pepper flakes and flaky salt; garnish with the dark green portions of the scallions. Serve with buttered toast.

Pesto scrambled eggs with fresh ricotta

In my fantasy life living on a farm, autumn would be dedicated to "putting things up." I'd pickle, can, preserve, dry, and freeze all the waning garden bounty before it succumbed to the first frost. In my Brooklyn reality, however, my garden gets just enough sun to nourish the few pots of herbs I try to remember to water. But that doesn't stop me from preserving my harvest to the utmost. Which means that come October, I make pesto for the freezer.

After a quick spin in the food processor, a jumble of bright green leaves, beige nuts, and dark oil becomes an emerald emulsion with a heady, herbal, garlicky fragrance that immediately fills the kitchen and makes your stomach growl. With it, I could make myself a hearty meal of pasta with pesto. But brunch is also appropriate, especially on a particular Sunday, giving me an excuse to make another of my pesto staples, softly scrambled eggs with pesto and cheese.

I vary the cheeses to match the contents of my refrigerator, using Cheddar, Gruyère, goat cheese, and even cream cheese with great success. On that day, the fridge yielded up some fresh ricotta.

After scrambling the eggs until they were barely set with large, quivering curds, I streaked in some freshly made pesto and dotted the top with ricotta. The ricotta, normally sweet and creamy, tasted even more so next to the salty, pungent pesto, and made a dense, luscious foil for the cloudlike eggs. It was a perfect meal that, thanks to my pesto stash, I'd get to enjoy all winter long.

Last of the summer pesto
makes about 1 cup

½ cup pine nuts

¾ cup extra-virgin olive oil

4 ounces fresh basil, stemmed (about 5 cups leaves)

2 or 3 garlic cloves, coarsely chopped

½ teaspoon salt, or to taste

1. Heat a small skillet over medium heat and add the pine nuts. Toast them, shaking the pan and stirring, until golden brown all over, about 3 minutes. Pour the nuts onto a plate to cool.

(continued)

2. Combine all the ingredients in a food processor or blender and puree until smooth. Use immediately, or transfer to an airtight container and store in the refrigerator for up to a week or in the freezer for up to 6 months.

Soft scrambled eggs with pesto and fresh ricotta
serves 2

1 tablespoon unsalted butter

5 large eggs

2 tablespoons grated Parmesan cheese (optional)

Pinch salt

Freshly ground black pepper, to taste

2 tablespoons pesto (recipe precedes), plus more to taste

⅓ cup fresh ricotta cheese, broken up into clumps

1. In a medium skillet, preferably well seasoned or nonstick, over medium-low heat, melt the butter.

2. In a medium bowl, beat the eggs, Parmesan (if using), salt, and pepper to taste. Pour the eggs into the pan, swirl, and reduce the heat to low. Using a heatproof rubber spatula, scramble the eggs until very loosely set and still runnier than you like them. Remove the pan from the heat and drizzle the pesto on top of the eggs. Give the eggs one more gentle scramble—enough to finish cooking them and to distribute the pesto somewhat—but do not overstir. The pesto should still be in dark green streaks, not homogenously combined with the eggs. Scatter the ricotta on top of the eggs and drizzle with more pesto, if desired. Serve at once.

Anya's potato and onion tortilla with allioli

When it comes to entertaining, my friend Anya von Bremzen goes all out. An invitation to her house for a "simple dinner with a few dear friends" means a buffet table overflowing with hors d'oeuvres, followed by several sit-down courses, then an extravagant dessert, maybe ice cream steeped with the dried rose petals she carted home from Istanbul.

Inevitably, I want to re-create her recipes, like her tender, eggy tortilla strewn with potatoes and topped with garlic *allioli*, the Spanish version of aioli or garlic mayonnaise. Luckily for me, chances are it's been published, as Anya has written several cookbooks. Indeed, a version of this is included in *The New Spanish Table*.

So I gave it a go, mixing and sautéing as per her expert instructions. When I turned the finished tortilla out of the pan, it was just solid enough to slice, but still soft and jiggly on the inside. I dolloped on a big glob of *allioli*, which is easily made by hand in 2 minutes with either a mortar and pestle or bowl and whisk. (It tends to separate when I use a blender.) The onions were both sweet and savory, and gave the tortilla a hearty, rich flavor. The potatoes were tender and toothsome and gave the eggs just enough substance without adding heft.

At Anya's, the tortilla was cut up and served with cocktails as an elegant finger-size tapas. But at home, with some hot buttered toast and jam, I'd just call it brunch.

If you have any left over, it's great cold the next day, eaten as is, or made into a sandwich with some of the *allioli* smeared on the bread.

serves 2 to 4

FOR THE ALLIOLI

1 garlic clove, minced

Pinch kosher salt

1 teaspoon freshly squeezed lemon juice

1 large egg yolk

½ cup extra-virgin olive oil

FOR THE TORTILLA

2 tablespoons unsalted butter

1 large Spanish onion, halved and thinly sliced

Kosher salt and freshly ground black pepper, to taste

1 cup cubed potato, cooked

8 large eggs, lightly beaten

2 tablespoons chopped fresh basil

(continued)

1. MAKE THE ALLIOLI: Using a mortar and pestle, pound the garlic and salt to make a paste. (Alternatively, you can use the flat of a knife to mash the garlic and salt on a cutting board until it becomes a paste, then transfer it to a medium bowl.)

2. Whisk in the lemon juice, then the egg yolk until thoroughly combined. While whisking or pounding constantly, slowly drizzle in the olive oil. It's best to have an extra pair of hands here; one person can whisk/pound while the other drizzles in the oil. Continue whisking until the oil is fully emulsified. If it seems too thick, drizzle in a few drops of hot water and mix well.

3. MAKE THE TORTILLA: Preheat the oven to 500°F.

4. In a large, preferably nonstick, ovenproof skillet over medium heat, melt the butter. Add the onion, season to taste with salt and pepper, and sauté until golden brown. Stir in the potato.

5. Reduce the heat to low. Using a heatproof spatula, mix in the eggs and basil. Cook, stirring with a spatula and pushing in the edges as they become firm so the liquid eggs run underneath the cooked, until the eggs are just set on the bottom but the top is still wet, about 5 minutes.

6. Place the skillet in the oven for about 3 minutes, or until the top of the tortilla is dry (do not overcook). Invert onto a plate and slice into wedges. Serve hot with dollops of the allioli.

Chic quiche

One day, I flipped through my old Julia Child cookbook and ran right into the quiche chapter.

"A quiche hot out of the oven, a salad, and a cool bottle of white wine—there's the perfect light meal," Julia wrote.

It is? I was intrigued. I was born too late to enjoy quiche's luscious '70s revival, and was exposed only to the unappetizing, broccoli-laden pies of the '80s. Her recipe for quiche Lorraine was as plain and chic as a little black dress—a homemade all-butter crust filled with heavy cream, eggs, bacon, and a dainty pinch of nutmeg. I soon finagled a quiche-making excuse by inviting a friend over for lunch, and whipped up Julia's recipe.

Well, sort of. What I did was merge her quiche Lorraine with her dainty *quiche au fromage*, imbued with Swiss cheese. As much as I wanted to embrace the ideal of culinary purity, I simply could not choose between the bacon and the cheese. So I used both.

But while the quiche baked, I had second thoughts, fearing my custard would be heavy and overcrowded instead of buoyant, jiggly, and silky as Julia described.

Once the center was just set, I cut two thick slices and my friend and I dug in. The custard was suffused with cheese flavor but was still light and satiny. And the nuggets of bacon added just the right salty-meaty note against the sweet, milky mellowness of the cream. It was still highly sophisticated, but maybe not to the plain-little-black-dress degree. Maybe instead to one spruced up, let's say, with a nice Hermès scarf.

serves 8

1 recipe piecrust (page 200)

All-purpose flour, for dusting

FOR THE QUICHE FILLING

1 large egg white

3 tablespoons grated Gruyère cheese (about ¾ ounce)

5 strips bacon (about 6 ounces), cut into ½-inch strips

3 large eggs

1½ cups heavy cream

¼ teaspoon freshly grated nutmeg

¼ teaspoon kosher salt

¼ teaspoon freshly ground black pepper

1 tablespoon unsalted butter, cubed

1. Preheat the oven to 375°F.

(continued)

2. On a lightly floured surface, roll the dough to a ⅜-inch thickness and press it into a 9-inch pie pan. Line the dough with foil and fill with pie weights, rice, or dried beans. Bake for 20 minutes, then remove the weights and foil and bake for 5 to 7 minutes more, until lightly golden.

3. Take the crust out of the oven and brush the bottom of the crust with the egg white, then sprinkle on the Gruyère in an even layer. Return the crust to the oven and bake for 10 to 13 minutes, until the cheese is lightly browned.

4. Meanwhile, in a large pan over medium heat, cook the bacon for 7 to 10 minutes, or until lightly browned but not yet crispy. Drain the bacon on a paper towel–lined plate.

5. In a medium bowl, whisk together the eggs, cream, nutmeg, salt, and pepper.

6. When the crust is lightly browned and the cheese has melted, sprinkle in the bacon pieces and carefully pour in the custard. Dot the top with the butter pieces and return to the oven. Bake for 25 to 35 minutes, until the top of the quiche is puffed up and golden and the middle is almost set. Allow to cool slightly, about 15 minutes, before serving.

Baked flounder and eggs

One Saturday morning, my friend Judith and I shopped for breakfast at the Greenpoint farmers' market. After we had acquired eggs, butter, cheese, fresh bread, and plenty of apples—the makings of a princely meal—Judith stopped at the fish stand, mentioning that her family often had fresh fish for breakfast when they vacationed at the North Sea in Holland.

Now, I know perfectly well that fish is a common breakfast staple all over the world, but fresh flounder for breakfast seemed exotic, at least to me.

Back in the kitchen, Judith simply swathed the fish in butter, salt, and pepper and broiled it, while I scrambled the eggs. There was nothing surprising about the flavors— the sweet, soft fish with its saline, buttery juices melding with fluffy farm-fresh eggs—but eaten all together, it was divine.

I could have stuck to Judith's original, gorgeously spare recipe. But my urge to embellish runs deep. So, for a garnish, I chopped together parsley, scallions, and capers to add a tangy, bright note and a little bit of color. Further, feeling lazy, I cracked the eggs directly into the roasting pan with the fish; if I timed it right, the yolks would stay runny and gush all over the flounder, creating a velvety sauce.

With its pungent green garnish adding verve and the yolks lending creaminess, it was a more complex dish than the original, but still an easy, quick change of pace for two on a weekend morning.

serves 2

3 tablespoons unsalted butter, melted

2 (8-ounce) boneless, skinless flounder fillets, rinsed and patted dry

¾ teaspoon kosher salt

½ teaspoon paprika

Freshly ground black pepper, to taste

4 large eggs

3 tablespoons chopped scallions (optional)

3 tablespoons chopped fresh parsley (optional)

1½ tablespoons drained capers, chopped (optional)

1. Preheat the oven to 400°F.

2. Pour the butter over the bottom of a 9 × 13-inch metal baking pan. Place the fish in the pan and turn to coat with the butter. Season with about half the salt and paprika and plenty of black pepper.

3. Bake for 2 to 4 minutes, then crack the eggs into the bottom of the pan in the corners; the eggs should land next to, not on top of, the fish. (If you like runny eggs, add them after 3 to 4 minutes; for medium-firm but still slightly runny eggs, add them after 2 minutes; and for very firm eggs, you can add them along with the fish at the beginning.) Season the eggs with the remaining salt and paprika, and more pepper. Bake until the fish is just opaque and the eggs are lightly set, 7 to 8 minutes more.

4. Meanwhile, in a small bowl, combine the scallions, parsley, and capers (if using). Transfer the fish and eggs to serving plates; garnish with the caper mixture, if you like.

Whole wheat biscuits with spicy cardamom butter

If there is only one thing I learned from writing cookbooks with various Southern food experts, including Paula Deen and Sylvia Woods, it is that if you're in the company of any good cook from the South, let them make the biscuits. They will probably be better at it than you. It's in their blood, in the way matzo brei is in mine.

That said, there are some tips to making truly light and flaky biscuits, the kind that break apart into buttery layers when you greedily pull the top off before smearing on even more butter (or gravy, if you're from the South).

The first is to use a light touch, making sure not to overmix the dough. You want to keep the butter in pieces as you would when making pie dough. Those little chunks melt in the oven, producing steam that creates the characteristic flakes. Another important biscuit rule is to go through whatever hoops necessary to serve them warm from the oven, slathered with even more butter.

I know my Southern friends will likely look askance at my whole wheat version. But I love the rich, roasty flavor of the whole wheat flour here, which makes the biscuits deeply complex but still wonderfully light. The cardamom butter, slightly sweet and very fragrant, is a nice match but purely optional. And if you've got homemade jam, such as the Rhubarb, Strawberry, and Lemon Marmalade on page 36, it will be most welcome here, with or without the cardamom butter.

serves 8

1 cup all-purpose flour, plus more for dusting

⅔ cup whole wheat flour

1½ tablespoons baking powder

¼ teaspoon kosher salt

6 tablespoons (¾ stick) cold unsalted butter, cubed, plus 1 tablespoon unsalted butter, melted

⅔ cup whole milk

1 tablespoon honey

Rhubarb, Strawberry, and Lemon Marmalade (page 36), or other jam (optional)

FOR THE SPICY CARDAMOM BUTTER

½ cup (1 stick) unsalted butter, at room temperature

1½ tablespoons honey, or more to taste

½ teaspoon ground cardamom, plus pinch more if it needs it

⅛ teaspoon kosher salt, or more to taste

⅛ teaspoon cayenne

1. Preheat the oven to 400°F. Line a rimmed baking sheet with parchment paper.

2. Place the flours, baking powder, and salt in a food processor and pulse to combine.

3. Add the cold butter and pulse until the mixture resembles coarse meal. Pour in the milk, drizzle in the honey, and continue pulsing until the dough starts to come together, scraping down the sides of the processor bowl if necessary.

4. Turn the dough out onto a lightly floured surface and gently pat it together. Use a floured biscuit cutter (2 to 3 inches in diameter) to cut out the biscuits. Transfer the biscuits to the prepared baking sheet, brush with the melted butter, and bake until golden brown, 15 to 18 minutes. Transfer the pan to a wire rack to cool for a few minutes (but not much longer) before serving.

5. While the biscuits are baking, prepare the cardamom butter by beating all the ingredients together with an electric mixer or in a food processor. Add more honey, salt, or spice to taste. Spread on the warm biscuits.

Double coconut granola

"Granola is really oatmeal cookies in disguise," my friend Robin always says.

I know exactly what she means. Granola is addictive in the same hard-to-stop-eating way as cookies, and when I have either in the house, I am completely and utterly at their mercy. Therefore, whenever I whip up a big batch of homemade granola, I only stash a little of it in the cupboard. The rest I pack up tightly in a jar and immediately hand off to Daniel so he can bring it to work (and far away from me). Otherwise, I am liable to scarf it down by the fistful and regret it later.

That said, if you can exercise more self-control, a batch of this is a good thing to keep in the pantry. It's very similar to my Olive Oil Granola (see page 26), with one major change: in place of the olive oil, I use virgin coconut oil. It makes for particularly crunchy oats with a deep coconut flavor that I play up by adding plenty of coconut chips to the mix. And virgin coconut oil is filled with lauric acid, which is also found in breast milk (you learn the darnedest things on the Internet), and which some research has shown both boosts the immune system and helps fight acne—though I suppose the acne part is for topical application. Not something you're likely to do with granola, no matter how addictive it is.

makes about 7 cups

3 cups old-fashioned rolled oats

1½ cups coarsely chopped raw pecans

1 cup hulled raw pumpkin seeds

1 cup coconut chips

½ cup pure maple syrup

½ cup virgin coconut oil, melted

⅓ cup packed light brown sugar

1 teaspoon kosher salt

½ teaspoon ground cinnamon

¼ teaspoon freshly grated nutmeg

¾ cup dried cherries

1. Preheat the oven to 300°F.

2. In a large bowl, combine the oats, pecans, pumpkin seeds, coconut chips, maple syrup, coconut oil, brown sugar, salt, cinnamon, and nutmeg. Spread the mixture on a rimmed baking sheet in an even layer and bake until golden all over, about 45 minutes, stirring every 10 minutes.

3. Transfer the granola to a large bowl and add the cherries, tossing to combine.

Olive oil granola with dried apricots and pistachios

There was a crowd of shoppers swarming at the back of BKLYN Larder. They hovered around a tray of free samples, gluttonously gobbling the contents. So I stuck my hand into the fray and nabbed a cup. It was granola, and the first bite was sweet and crunchy. But then the salt hit me, followed by something savory and almost bitter; the combo was addictive. The secret ingredient, said the label, was olive oil.

When I have made granola, it's usually been slicked with a neutral oil such as saf-flower, which helps crisp the oats but does nothing for the flavor. Using good extra-virgin olive oil, along with a hefty dose of salt, was a brilliant twist.

I decided to make a batch of my own, at home. But first, I called Nekisia Davis, the owner of Early Bird Foods & Co., to see if she'd divulge the recipe. She gave me the pro-portions, emphasizing that it's the balance of sweet and salty that makes her granola like health-conscious crack. Using olive oil was an easy decision—she said she puts it in everything. I substituted pistachios for pecans, nixed the sunflower seeds, and added cinnamon and cardamom to complement the apricots.

I mixed the cooled granola into a bowl of ripe berries, dabbing the top with milky ricotta. I lapped it up and yearned for more. But that was no problem. With two quarts in the cupboard and the recipe on hand, I knew I'd be eating granola all summer long—unless the hungry hordes find out where I live.

makes about 9 cups

3 cups old-fashioned rolled oats

1½ cups shelled raw pistachios

1 cup hulled raw pumpkin seeds

1 cup coconut chips

¾ cup pure maple syrup (you can use ⅔ cup, but the granola will be drier)

½ cup extra-virgin olive oil

⅓ cup packed light brown sugar

1 teaspoon kosher salt

½ teaspoon ground cinnamon

½ teaspoon ground cardamom or ground ginger

¾ cup chopped dried apricots

Fresh ricotta cheese, for serving

Fresh berries, for serving

1. Preheat the oven to 300°F.

2. In a large bowl, combine the oats, pistachios, pumpkin seeds, coconut chips, maple syrup, olive oil, brown sugar, salt, cinnamon, and cardamom. Spread the mixture on a large rimmed baking sheet in an even layer and bake for 45 minutes, stirring every 10 minutes, until golden brown and well toasted.

3. Transfer the granola to a large bowl and add the apricots, tossing to combine. Serve with ricotta and berries, if desired.

Baked apples with fig and cardamom crumble

Here's what I love about apple crumble: the crumbly, cinnamon-sweet topping. Here's what I don't love about apple crumble: the mushy, applesauce-like fruit at the bottom.

This recipe fixes the mush factor without compromising the crumbly bits on top. My trick is to quarter rather than slice the apples. The larger pieces won't break down as quickly or as much, but they do soften to a luscious spoonable-ness. Bigger apple pieces also make the dish easier and faster to put together.

The last time I made apple crumble, I also threw in some dried figs plumped in brandy to give the dish pockets of sweet, chewy goodness. Feel free to leave them out if you don't like dried figs. Or substitute a dried fruit that you do like. Dried apricot slices, cherries, and cranberries would be marvelous and very pretty.

This is a fine brunch or breakfast dish with a ratio of apple crumble to yogurt in favor of the yogurt. Ice cream, especially a slightly exotic flavor such as ginger or green tea, would make this into a homey but dinner party–suitable dessert.

serves 6 to 8

FOR THE FRUIT

3 tablespoons brandy

1 cup dried figs, coarsely chopped

4 large apples (about 3 pounds), peeled, quartered, and cored

2 tablespoons granulated sugar

2 teaspoons freshly squeezed lemon juice

½ teaspoon ground cardamom

2 tablespoons unsalted butter, melted

FOR THE CRUMBLE TOPPING

½ cup all-purpose flour

¼ cup plus 3 tablespoons packed light brown sugar

¼ cup whole wheat flour

¼ cup old-fashioned rolled oats

¾ teaspoon ground cardamom

½ teaspoon ground ginger

⅛ teaspoon kosher salt

¾ cup (1½ sticks) cold unsalted butter, cut into pieces

Greek yogurt, for serving

1. Preheat the oven to 375°F. Lightly grease a 9-inch-square baking pan.

2. PREPARE THE FRUIT: In a small saucepan, bring the brandy to a simmer. Take it off the heat, add the chopped figs, and cover the pan. Allow the figs to plump in the liquid for 30 minutes.

3. In a large bowl, toss the apples with the granulated sugar, lemon juice, and cardamom. Add the melted butter and toss again until the apples are coated. Stir in the figs along with any unabsorbed brandy.

4. MAKE THE CRUMBLE TOPPING: In a bowl, mix together the all-purpose flour, brown sugar, whole wheat flour, oats, cardamom, ginger, and salt. Add the butter pieces and mix in with your fingers or a fork until large crumbs form.

5. Scrape the apple mixture into the prepared pan and top with an even layer of the crumble. Bake until the apples are tender and the topping is golden brown, 45 to 50 minutes. Transfer the pan to a wire rack to cool slightly, 15 to 20 minutes. Serve warm if you can, with Greek yogurt.

Rhubarb "big crumb" coffee cake

Rhubarb is an alarmingly sour vegetable passed off as a fruit but requiring a huge mound of sugar to effect the transformation.

Crumb cake is a huge mound of sugar disguised as a cake but demanding a bracing counterpoint—say, a swallow of coffee or tea—to allay its cloying sweetness. These two truths coexisted in my mind without overlapping until I bit into a piece of crumb cake so texturally perfect yet so toothachingly sweet that the only antidote was sucking on the lemon from my glass of seltzer.

The sourness of the lemon immediately made me think about the rhubarb I had in the fridge. Why not mix the rhubarb into a crumb cake to cut the cake's sweetness?

Using a technique from Claudia Fleming (I wrote a cookbook with her when she was at Gramercy Tavern), I tossed the rhubarb in just a bit of sugar, which encourages the sturdy stems to absorb the syrup that forms. Though I was loath to add more sugar to a recipe that was already overloaded, I did it anyway, as I knew it worked in Claudia's rhubarb crisp. Then, with a trick lifted from *Cook's Illustrated* magazine, I made a homogeneous brown sugar dough and pinched off marbles to form big crumbs for the topping.

When my rhubarb crumb cake cooled, I dug in. The rhubarb was mellow and gently sweet, with still enough zesty bite to offset the sugary cake and grape-size crumbs. At last I had crumb cake fulfillment. Which just goes to show: When less isn't more, try adding more.

serves 8

FOR THE RHUBARB FILLING

½ pound rhubarb, trimmed and cut into ½-inch-thick slices

¼ cup granulated sugar

2 teaspoons cornstarch

½ teaspoon ground ginger

FOR THE BIG CRUMBS

⅓ cup packed dark brown sugar

⅓ cup granulated sugar

1 teaspoon ground cinnamon

½ teaspoon ground ginger

⅛ teaspoon salt

½ cup (1 stick) unsalted butter, melted

1¾ cups cake flour

FOR THE CAKE

⅓ cup sour cream

1 large egg

1 large egg yolk

2 teaspoons vanilla extract

1 cup cake flour

½ cup granulated sugar

½ teaspoon baking soda

½ teaspoon baking powder

¼ teaspoon salt

6 tablespoons (¾ stick) unsalted butter, cut into 8 pieces, at room temperature

1. Preheat the oven to 325°F. Grease an 8-inch-square baking pan.

2. MAKE THE FILLING: In a large bowl, toss together the rhubarb, granulated sugar, cornstarch, and ginger. Let macerate while you prepare the crumbs and cake.

3. MAKE THE CRUMBS: In a large bowl, whisk together the sugars, spices, salt, and melted butter until smooth. Stir in the flour with a spatula. It will look like a solid dough.

4. MAKE THE CAKE: In a small bowl, stir together the sour cream, egg, egg yolk, and vanilla. In the bowl of an electric mixer fitted with the paddle attachment, mix together the flour, granulated sugar, baking soda, baking powder, and salt. Add the butter and a spoonful of the sour cream mixture and mix on medium speed until all the flour is moistened. Increase the speed and beat for 30 seconds. Add the remaining sour cream mixture in two batches, beating for 20 seconds and scraping down the sides of the bowl with a spatula after each addition. Scoop out about ½ cup of the batter and set aside.

5. Scrape the remaining batter into the prepared pan. Spoon the rhubarb over the batter. Dollop the remaining batter over the rhubarb (it doesn't have to be even).

6. Using your fingers, break the topping mixture into big crumbs, ½ inch to ¾ inch in size. They don't have to be uniform; just make sure the majority are around that size. Sprinkle the crumbs over the cake. Bake the cake until a toothpick inserted into the center comes out clean (it might be moist from the rhubarb), 45 to 55 minutes. Let cool completely before serving.

St. Mark's gooey honey butter cake with lemon and cinnamon

There was one man ahead of me at the Made By Molly stand at the Park Slope farmers' market, and one piece of St. Louis Gooey Butter Cake left. And the man ordered it. After I groaned loudly, he agreed to give it to me in exchange for a brownie and two coconut bars. It was well worth it.

Not wanting to wait another week, I asked Molly Killeen to share her recipe. It started with a yeast dough, which she found New Yorkers preferred, as a way to cut down on the cloying sweetness (they often use a butter cake in St. Louis). She topped the crust with a treacly, mysterious alchemy of butter, sugar, and eggs. After baking, it had a dense, curd-like layer, similar to pecan pie but firmer, with a buttery, crackling crust on top.

The next time I made it, I substituted honey for the corn syrup and added a lot of grated lemon zest, because ever since my first Luden's cough drop, I've always loved the combination of lemon and honey. I also mixed some cinnamon into the crust, hoping it would bring out the warm, toasty quality of the yeast dough.

With its caramelized notes and vivid citrus nuance, I liked my cake even better than the original. I rechristened it St. Mark's Gooey Cake, after my cross street in Brooklyn, where I now make the cake any time I get a craving, no negotiations required.

serves 8 to 12

FOR THE CRUST

3 tablespoons milk, at room temperature

1¾ teaspoons active dry yeast

6 tablespoons (¾ stick) unsalted butter, at room temperature

3 tablespoons sugar

2 teaspoons ground cinnamon (optional)

1 teaspoon kosher salt

1 large egg

1¾ cups all-purpose flour

FOR THE TOPPING

3 tablespoons plus 1 teaspoon honey (or use corn syrup)

2½ teaspoons vanilla extract

¾ cup (1½ sticks) unsalted butter, at room temperature

1½ cups sugar

½ teaspoon kosher salt

1 large egg

Finely grated zest of 1 lemon (about 1 tablespoon; optional)

1 cup plus 3 tablespoons all-purpose flour

Confectioners' sugar, for sprinkling (optional)

1. MAKE THE CRUST: In a small bowl, mix together the milk with 2 tablespoons lukewarm water. Add the yeast and whisk gently until it dissolves. The mixture should foam slightly.

2. In the bowl of an electric mixer fitted with the paddle attachment, cream the butter, sugar, cinnamon (if using), and salt. Scrape down the sides of the bowl and beat in the egg. Alternately add the flour and the milk mixture, scraping down the sides of the bowl between each addition. Beat the dough on medium speed until it forms a smooth mass and pulls away from the sides of the bowl, 7 to 10 minutes.

3. Press the dough into an ungreased 9 × 13-inch baking dish at least 2 inches deep. Cover the dish with plastic wrap or a clean dishtowel and set aside in a warm, dry place to rise until doubled, 2½ to 3 hours.

4. When the dough is almost ready, preheat the oven to 350°F.

5. MAKE THE TOPPING: In a small bowl, mix together the honey, 2 tablespoons water, and the vanilla. In the bowl of an electric mixer fitted with the paddle attachment, cream the butter, sugar, and salt until light and fluffy, 5 to 7 minutes. Scrape down the sides of the bowl and beat in the egg and lemon zest. Alternately add the flour and the honey mixture, scraping down the sides of the bowl between each addition.

6. Spoon the topping in large dollops over the risen crust and use a spatula to gently spread it into an even layer. Bake for 35 to 45 minutes. The cake will rise and fall in waves in the dish with a golden brown top but will still be liquid inside when done. Let cool in the pan before sprinkling with confectioners' sugar, if desired, and serving.

note: If you'd rather cling to tradition, omit the lemon zest and use corn syrup in place of honey.

Maple blueberry cake

It takes a tremendous amount of willpower for me to bake this cake. Whenever I bring home a pint of blueberries from the market, I immediately gobble them all up, aided by Dahlia, who loves blueberries best, despite the fact that she can't stick them onto her fingers like hats, raspberry style. Leaving some for cake or crisp or anything that requires forethought seems nearly impossible when the plump, fleshy berries are in the room.

Of course I do have a few tricks I can pull out when necessary. So when I decided I wanted to make a blueberry loaf cake, I bought an extra pint of the berries and hid it in the back of the fridge behind the eggs until I was ready to bake.

By the time I pulled out the pint a few days later, it had been reduced by about half (turns out Daniel especially loves blueberries in his smoothies). Luckily, there were still just enough for cake.

I added whole wheat flour to the batter of my usual buttery loaf cake recipe to give it richness and cut some of the sweetness of the cake itself. The result was a moist, fine-crumbed loaf with plenty of jammy purple pockets, well worth the delayed berry gratification to bake.

Raspberries, cubed nectarines, or peaches can stand in for the blueberries. Or use a combination of fruit if your family hasn't saved you enough of any one.

makes 1 (8-inch) loaf cake

¾ cup plus 2 tablespoons all-purpose flour

¾ cup plus 2 tablespoons whole wheat flour

1½ teaspoons baking powder

¼ teaspoon baking soda

¼ teaspoon kosher salt

⅔ cup pure maple syrup, preferably Grade B

1 large egg, lightly beaten

½ cup milk

6 tablespoons (¾ stick) unsalted butter, melted

1 cup fresh blueberries

1. Preheat the oven to 400°F. Lightly grease an 8-inch loaf pan.

2. In a large bowl, combine the flours, baking powder, baking soda, and salt.

3. In a separate bowl, whisk together the maple syrup, egg, milk, and melted butter. Pour the maple syrup mixture into the flour mixture and fold together until just combined. Gently fold in the blueberries. Pour the batter into the prepared pan. Bake until golden brown and a toothpick inserted into the center comes out clean, 50 to 60 minutes.

4. Transfer the cake to a wire rack set over a rimmed baking sheet; let cool completely. Once cool, run the tip of a knife or an offset spatula around the edges of the pan to loosen the cake. Place a plate over the pan. Flip the cake onto the plate. Tap the sides and bottom of the pan to help release the cake (the berries might have gotten stuck, and this helps unstick them). Remove the pan. Turn the cake right-side up and put it on the baking sheet. Slice and serve.

Rhubarb, strawberry, and lemon marmalade

This is what I do with springtime strawberries that aren't pretty enough to sit on top of a tart. I make them into jam, adding rhubarb and a little lemon to brighten their intense sweetness.

I got the basic technique for this jam from the French jam-making guru Christine Ferber. She makes the most incredible jams I've ever tasted, and I adopted her cookbook *Mes Confitures* as my preserving bible.

At first, however, I was skeptical about the need to macerate the fruit overnight in sugar. Can't one just boil it longer and not bother? But having made jams both ways, I can tell you that macerating really does make a huge difference in texture. It allows the fruit to candy and absorb some of the sugar before it hits the heat, which helps it maintain its texture rather than falling apart to mush.

This recipe gives you a translucent, lemony jelly packed with candied chunks of strawberry and rhubarb. It's excellent on toast or biscuits (page 22), though I often find myself eating it off the spoon in winter when I want a sugary treat that reminds me of the sweetness of spring.

makes about 6 cups

1¼ pounds rhubarb, washed, trimmed, and diced (about 4½ cups)

1½ pounds strawberries, washed, trimmed, and diced (about 6 cups)

4½ cups sugar

Finely grated zest of 1 lemon

Freshly squeezed juice of ½ lemon

4 to 6 sterilized jam jars, depending upon size (see Note)

1. In a large bowl, place the rhubarb, strawberries, sugar, lemon zest, and lemon juice. Cover and let sit, stirring occasionally, for 6 to 8 hours or up to overnight.

2. Put a small plate or saucer in the freezer. Place a sieve over a large saucepan and pour the fruit mixture into the sieve, reserving the fruit for later. Affix a candy thermometer to the side of the saucepan and place the pan over medium-high heat. Bring the mixture to a boil, then reduce the heat to to medium-low and simmer until the temperature reads 230°F, 15 to 20 minutes.

3. Add the reserved fruit and bring the mixture back to a boil, stirring occasionally. Reduce the heat to medium-low. Simmer for 5 to 10 minutes. Check to see if the jam will set by placing a small spoonful on the chilled saucer. Push the edge of the jam puddle inward with your finger; if the puddle wrinkles, then the jam is done.

4. Ladle the hot jam into the sterilized jars, leaving ½ inch of headspace, and seal tightly. If you want to can the jars, process in a canner according to the manufacturer's directions. Or, for shorter storage, turn the sealed jars upside down and allow them to cool to room temperature (see Note). The jar tops should be sealed and look concave. Properly sealed jars will keep in the refrigerator for at least several months or in the pantry for at least several weeks. If any jars don't seal, store them in the fridge and use them up first.

note: I never can my jams with a pressure canner, preferring instead to make small batches of jam and use them up quickly. This is my method. (Please note that this does not comply with the USDA recommendations for safe canning.) If you have a dishwasher, wash the jars and lids (use the sterilize setting if your dishwasher has one) and take them out while they're still hot. Or you can boil the jars and the lids for 10 minutes. Set them upside down on a clean dishtowel to dry. Ladle the hot jam into the hot jars, leaving ½ inch of headspace, and screw on the lids while everything is still steaming hot. Turn them upside-down and allow a vacuum seal to occur. You will know the jars are sealed if the tops of the jars look concave. This will preserve them for weeks and probably months. If you see mold, toss the jam. Note that botulism isn't an issue with jam-making because of the high acid and sugar content, so you don't need to worry about that. But moldy jam isn't tasty.

If you don't feel like dealing with any of this, just store the jam in the fridge and use it up in the next few months. Or pop it into the freezer for longer storage.

lunch
AND OTHER LIGHT MEALS

Cantaloupe and yogurt soup with toasted cumin salt

I came up with this cool, refreshing soup on one of the sweatiest, stickiest, steamiest lunchtimes of summer, too darn hot to do *anything* at all, let alone chew. Whatever I had for lunch would have to be blended into liquid submission, and my first thought was to make an icy fruit smoothie. But I was craving salt, something potato chip–salty, in sippable form.

I remembered a bracing Indian yogurt drink called a lassi. Frothed up from yogurt, salt, ice, and sometimes lemon juice and/or cumin, it's salty, filling, and ridiculously easy, a perfect summer lunch.

I whirled one together and while it was cold and zippy enough to quell my cravings, it could have used a sweet element to balance out the yogurt tanginess. I poked around in the fridge and unearthed a bowl of cut-up cantaloupe and half a jalapeño. I threw them both in the blender bowl. My new creation was earthy from the cumin, fruity, and very creamy, with a gentle bite from the pepper. It was far too heady and complex to sip through a straw, so I moved it to a bowl and took up a spoon.

Soon the blender was empty and my belly was full. Happily, there were many weeks of summer left, which meant many sticky, sweaty days and all the good liquid food that went with them.

serves 4 to 6

2 pounds peeled and cubed cantaloupe (8 cups)	2 teaspoons freshly squeezed lemon juice
1 cup plain yogurt	½ teaspoon kosher salt
½ to 1 jalapeño, to taste, seeded and finely chopped	1 teaspoon cumin seeds
	2 teaspoons coarse sea salt

1. Combine the cantaloupe, yogurt, jalapeño, lemon juice, and kosher salt in a blender and puree until smooth. Pour into a bowl, cover tightly with plastic wrap, and chill for 1 hour.

2. In a small skillet over medium heat, toast the cumin seeds until fragrant, about 1 minute. Pour into a mortar and pestle and add the coarse sea salt. Pound the mixture a few times until the cumin seeds are lightly crushed. (If you don't have a mortar and pestle, put the cumin and salt onto a cutting board and either smack it with the side of a heavy cleaver or knife, or roll over them with a rolling pin or the side of a wine bottle.)

3. To serve, ladle the soup into individual bowls. Garnish with the cumin salt.

Red lentil soup with lemon

Once, at a dinner party of my friend Anya, little white espresso cups filled with some kind of steaming liquid were passed around as hors d'oeuvres. Deep in conversation, I took an absent-minded sip that instantly dazzled me: a gorgeous soup, possessing a velvety texture and a zesty, spicy flavor.

It was her red lentil soup, and I was smitten. After a moderate amount of pleading, Anya promised to send me the recipe the next day.

As I figured from that small portion, the ingredient list called for broth, onion, cumin, garlic, lemons, chili powder, and red lentils, which cook faster than brown or green lentils and don't hold their shape well—ideal for soup. Then came some surprises: dried mint, fresh tomatoes, and bulgur—none of which were in my cupboard at the moment.

As determined as I was to make that soup, I was equally determined not to leave the house. Instead of tomatoes, I used a fat dollop of tomato paste and a chopped carrot to compensate for the lost vegetable matter and ruddy color. The bulgur was a harder swap-out, so I left it out altogether and doubled the lentils. Half an hour later, my lentil soup was bubbling hot and ready. To substitute for the mint, I floated a handful of chopped cilantro over the surface.

Lighter and brothier, my version had a buoyant, lemony disposition grounded by a profound cumin-and-chili backbone.

Even better, if I kept a supply of red lentils around, I could make the soup in under an hour whenever my heart desired. And I've been making it ever since.

serves 6

¼ cup olive oil

2 large onions, chopped

4 garlic cloves, minced

2 tablespoons tomato paste

2 teaspoons ground cumin

½ teaspoon kosher salt, plus more to taste

½ teaspoon freshly ground black pepper

Pinch chili powder or cayenne, plus more to taste

2 quarts chicken broth or vegetable broth

2 cups red lentils

2 large carrots, diced

Freshly squeezed juice of 1 lemon, or more to taste

⅓ cup chopped fresh cilantro, mint, or parsley

Good olive oil, for drizzling

1. In a large pot over high heat, heat the oil until hot and shimmering. Add the onions and garlic and sauté until golden, about 4 minutes.

2. Stir in the tomato paste, cumin, salt, pepper, and chili powder and sauté for 2 minutes more.

3. Add the broth, 2 cups water, the lentils, and the carrots. Bring to a simmer, then partially cover the pot and reduce the heat to medium-low. Simmer until the lentils are soft, about 30 minutes. Taste and add more salt if necessary.

4. Using an immersion or regular blender or a food processor, puree half the soup (it should be somewhat chunky, not smooth).

5. Reheat the soup if necessary, then stir in the lemon juice and cilantro, mint, or parsley. Serve the soup drizzled with good olive oil and dusted very lightly with chili powder, if desired.

Curried coconut tomato soup

A play on cream of tomato soup, this recipe is supremely satisfying for the dairy-avoidant set (in other words, I can feed this to my husband).

It's just the thing to serve on those raw April days when it feels like March outside the door. Since this soup doesn't rely on any fresh produce, barring an onion and a little green garnish, you could even make it in winter, where it would be as welcome as the first warm breezes of spring.

The curry powder, boosted with coriander and cumin, adds an earthy, fragrant note that you definitely don't find in a can of Campbell's, and the coconut milk makes the whole thing ever so slightly sweet. It's a thinner, brothier soup than the cream-based cream of tomato soups you usually find. But I like it all the better for this because I can eat more of it before filling up. It's got a flavor you won't want to end at the bottom of just one bowl.

To turn this into a full meal, add a few handfuls of peeled small shrimp, fish chunks, or bay scallops to the soup during the last 5 minutes of cooking, and serve with rice or orzo.

serves 2 to 4

2 tablespoons unsalted butter	½ teaspoon ground cumin
1 Spanish onion, thinly sliced	Pinch chili powder
1½ teaspoons kosher salt, plus more to taste	1 (28-ounce) can diced or whole peeled plum tomatoes
1½ teaspoons curry powder	2 (13.5-ounce) cans coconut milk
½ teaspoon ground coriander	Chopped fresh cilantro, mint, or basil, for garnish

1. In a large saucepan over medium heat, melt the butter. Add the onion and ½ teaspoon of the salt. Reduce the heat to medium-low, cover, and cook, stirring occasionally, until the onion is meltingly tender, about 15 minutes. Reduce the heat and add a sprinkle of water if necessary to keep the onion from browning.

2. Stir in the curry powder, coriander, cumin, and chili powder and cook for 1 minute. Stir in the tomatoes and their juice and 4 cups water. Bring the mixture to a simmer over medium-high heat. Simmer, uncovered, for 20 minutes.

(continued)

3. Working in batches, transfer the soup to a blender and puree until smooth. Return the soup to the pan. Whisk in 1 can of the coconut milk. Spoon off ½ cup cream from the top of the second can (reserve the remaining milk for another use, such as Coconut Rice, page 144) and whisk it into the soup. Stir in the remaining 1 teaspoon salt. Gently heat the soup over medium-low heat for 10 minutes, or until it reaches the desired consistency. Ladle the soup into bowls and garnish with cilantro or other herbs to your taste.

Spicy chicken barley soup with sweet potato and spinach

I grew up eating mushroom barley soup in my grandma Ella's kitchen on her red Formica-topped table: homey, scented with garlic and herbs, and loaded with carrots and celery.

Once, on a gray and rainy autumn day, I wanted the barley and I wanted soup, but I didn't want the same old barley soup. I wanted something to transport me somewhere else, somewhere sunny and hot where flannel-lined raincoats are unheard of and sweet-smelling spices are used with an open hand.

I thought back to a North African–inspired soup I once made, with chicken, chickpeas, and sweet potato, and a deep, ruddy broth filled with ginger, chili powder, and paprika. I could use this basic recipe as a template, swapping out barley for the chickpeas and adding spinach for contrast.

Because pearl barley takes about an hour and a half to cook through, I added the sweet potato thirty minutes after the barley had been simmering. After another forty minutes, both the barley and the sweet potato were soft and supple and infused with spices, as were the bite-size pieces of chicken I added at the end.

Brightened with lemon and cilantro to finish, it wasn't a soup my grandmother would have ever met, and I'm sad I can no longer introduce them. I know she would have loved it as much as I do.

serves 6 to 8

3 tablespoons extra-virgin olive oil

1 Spanish onion, chopped

1 teaspoon kosher salt (see Note), plus more to taste

½ teaspoon sweet paprika

¼ teaspoon ground cinnamon

¼ teaspoon chili powder

¼ teaspoon ground coriander

¼ teaspoon freshly ground black pepper

Pinch cayenne

1 tablespoon tomato paste

3 garlic cloves, chopped

6 cups low-sodium or good homemade chicken broth (see Note)

1 cup pearl barley, rinsed well

1 sweet potato, peeled and diced

12 ounces boneless, skinless chicken breasts or thighs, cut into bite-size pieces

1 (5-ounce) bag baby spinach

½ cup chopped fresh cilantro or mint, plus more for garnish

1 tablespoon freshly squeezed lemon juice

Lemon wedges, for serving

(continued)

1. In a large soup pot over high heat, heat the oil. Add the onion and salt and sauté until limp, about 3 minutes. Add all the spices and sauté until fragrant, about 2 minutes. Add the tomato paste and sauté for another minute, until darkened but not burned. (If the tomato paste gets too dark too quickly, reduce the heat.)

2. Add the garlic and sauté for 1 minute more.

3. Return the heat to high if you lowered it, then add the broth, 2 cups water, and the barley to the pot. Bring to a boil, then reduce the heat to simmer for 30 minutes. Add the sweet potato and cook until the barley and sweet potato are soft, 30 minutes to 1 hour more, adding more water to the pot if necessary (it should not get too thick; this is soup, not stew). Add the chicken, partially cover the pot, reduce the heat to medium-low, and simmer for 10 minutes.

4. Add the spinach and cilantro or mint to the pot and simmer until the spinach is wilted, about 5 minutes more. Stir in the lemon juice and more salt, if desired. Serve garnished with cilantro or mint with lemon wedges alongside.

note: If your chicken broth is on the salty side, reduce the salt to ½ teaspoon to start. You can always add more salt later.

Creamy parsnip and leek soup with bacon

Bone-chilling, damp days and frosty nights bellow for soup, so in February we eat pots upon pots of it. And one of my favorite midweek, postwork, didn't-plan-anything-else-for-dinner soups to throw together is a simple root vegetable puree.

My technique never varies, and it always produces something good and heartwarming to eat.

I start with a sautéed base of alliums (onion, shallot, leek, garlic, whatever-have-you) and add whatever root vegetables are starting to soften in the bin, some kind of seasonings (herbs, spices), and plenty of good, preferably homemade, broth (or water seasoned with a lot of salt and pepper). Then I let everything simmer until the roots are spoonably soft. The final puree is as creamy and comforting as mashed potatoes, but eminently more meal-like and satisfying.

The parsnips and leeks in this version make it sweeter and milder than most, so I like to pair it with something bright flavored and bold. Crusty dark bread, toasted and rubbed with garlic, is a simple, crunchy, bold contrast to the pale suppleness of the soup. A simple salad of whatever greens you've got will round out your meal.

serves 4 to 6

4 to 6 tablespoons (½ to ¾ stick) unsalted butter

4 large leeks, white and light green parts only, cleaned and sliced (see Note)

1 teaspoon kosher salt, plus more to taste

Freshly ground black pepper, to taste

4 large celery stalks, with leaves

4 fresh thyme sprigs

1 bay leaf

Parsley stems, if you've got them (optional)

1¼ pounds parsnips, sliced

1 pound potatoes (2 or 3 small ones), peeled and cut into chunks

1 quart chicken broth or vegetable broth

Few drops freshly squeezed lemon juice (optional)

Thick slices pumpernickel or other hearty bread, for serving

1 garlic clove, halved

Good olive oil, for drizzling

Urfa or Aleppo pepper flakes, for garnish (optional)

(continued)

1. In a soup pot over medium heat, melt the butter, then add the leeks, salt, and plenty of black pepper and sauté gently until the leeks are softened, about 5 minutes.

2. Meanwhile, slice the celery, reserving the leaves. Add the celery to the pot and sauté for 5 minutes more, until the leeks are lightly golden around the edges and the celery is shiny.

3. If you've got kitchen twine, tie the thyme, bay leaf, and celery leaves into a bundle (you could also add parsley stems here if you like). Throw it into the pot (if you don't have twine, just throw in the herbs, but you will have to fish them out later) along with the parsnips, potatoes, and broth. Add 2 cups water and bring everything to a simmer; cook until the vegetables are perfectly soft without any hard bits, 30 to 45 minutes.

4. Pluck out and discard the herbs or herb bundle. Puree the soup, adding a little water if it seems too thick. Add more salt to taste and some lemon juice if the flavor seems a little flat.

5. To serve, toast the bread, then rub with the garlic halves and drizzle with good olive oil. Ladle the soup into bowls and garnish with good olive oil and pepper flakes.

note: To clean leeks, slice them in half lengthwise. Holding each leek half under a running tap, let the water slide between the leek layers, swishing out any soil hidden there.

Ham bone, greens, and bean soup

I've made ham hock soup, I've made bacon soup, and I've made soup with a diced-up pig's ear. But I doubt I would ever have made ham bone soup if I hadn't taken a liking to the name, which I spotted while flipping through an old Junior League cookbook one day.

The soup sounded so . . . well, bare bones, which intrigued me, as I imagined a pot swirling with nothing but water and several cartoonish white bones in it, the bony version of stone soup.

And just as stone soup is actually made of vegetables, so is ham bone soup. Most recipes call for beans, greens, onions, carrots—ingredients that would make any soup taste good, with or without the bones and stones.

However, unlike the stone in stone soup, which adds nothing to the vegetables in the pot, the ham bone makes the soup. It not only benefits from the bone's meaty, smoky flavor, but the broth gains body and richness from all the luscious marrow.

It's an excellent soup, flavorful, rich, easy to make, and filled with tender beans and an array of seasonal vegetables that you can vary with what's available. But no matter what you do, strive to include the cabbage, which, cooked for almost an hour, softens into translucent, marrow-imbued bits that melt on the tongue.

serves 6 to 8

1 cup dried pinto beans	1 bay leaf
4 strips bacon, cut into ½-inch pieces	2½ teaspoons salt, plus more to taste
3 large carrots, diced	½ head green cabbage, shredded (about 8 cups)
2 celery stalks, diced	1 bunch kale, stems removed and leaves chopped into bite-size pieces
1 large onion, diced	
3 garlic cloves, finely chopped	Freshly ground black pepper, to taste
1 ham bone (1¼ pounds), cut in half or thirds (ask your butcher to do this for you)	Hot sauce or apple cider vinegar, for serving

1. Soak the beans in plenty of cold water overnight. If you don't have that much time, you can use the quick-soak method: In a large pot, bring the beans and plenty of cold water to a boil. Turn off the heat, cover the pot, and let stand for 1 hour. Drain the beans.

(continued)

2. Heat a large pot over medium-high heat. Add the bacon and cook until crisp, 5 to 7 minutes; remove with a slotted spoon to a paper towel–lined plate and save for garnishing the soup. Add the carrots, celery, and onion to the bacon fat in the pan. Cook, stirring, until softened, about 5 minutes. Add the garlic and cook for 1 minute.

3. Drop the ham bone and bay leaf into the pot and add 8 cups water and the salt. Bring the mixture to a boil over high heat; add the beans, reduce the heat to medium-low, and simmer for 30 minutes. Stir in the cabbage and simmer for 30 minutes. Stir in the kale and simmer until the kale is soft but still vibrantly green, about 15 minutes. If you're like me, you'll want to remove the meat and delicious fatty bits from the ham bone, chop them up, and stir them back into the soup. Season with pepper, a dash of hot sauce or vinegar, and more salt, if needed. Crumble the bacon on top.

Corn salad with tomatoes, avocados, and lime cilantro dressing

Even more so than corn on the cob swabbed with butter, when summer comes, I look forward to sweet, nubby corn salads loaded with vegetables and a zesty dressing.

This one is my favorite of many corn salad possibilities, mostly because of the creaminess of the avocado. It's so softly pleasant on the tongue next to all those crunchy corn kernels and juicy bits of tomato. You can even use leftover boiled or grilled corn—just slice off the kernels, no additional cooking required.

It's the perfect party salad because you can make it ahead and it can sit out all day without wilting. But once it hits the table, I guarantee it won't last long. It's just the kind of thing that people go nuts for, no matter what else is on offer.

serves 4 to 6

Kernels from 3 ears corn

2 tablespoons freshly squeezed lime juice

2 garlic cloves, finely chopped

½ teaspoon kosher salt, plus more to taste

½ teaspoon freshly ground black pepper

¼ cup extra-virgin olive oil

1 large tomato, diced

2 ripe avocados, pitted, peeled, and diced

2 scallions, finely chopped

¼ cup chopped fresh cilantro

1. Bring a medium pot of water to a boil. Drop in the corn and cook until just tender, about 2 minutes. Drain.

2. In a bowl, whisk together the lime juice, garlic, salt, and pepper. Whisk in the oil.

3. In a large bowl, combine the corn, tomato, avocados, scallions, and cilantro. Add the dressing and toss well to coat. Serve immediately.

Israeli couscous with fresh corn, tomatoes, and feta

Whole wheat Israeli couscous is technically pasta—semolina flour and water rolled into little pasta balls. (Regular couscous is even tinier pasta balls, by the way.) But whenever I contemplate what to do with it, I consider it a grain—a fast-cooking, nubby little grain that's as fat and round as barley (though less starchy) and as earthy tasting as farro (though less chewy).

Usually, I just serve it as a side dish for saucy sautés, the kind with lots of pan juices for the couscous to absorb. But I also like it in this colorful summery dish, which is a cross between a warm salad and a pilaf. Folding the corn and tomato into the couscous while it is still warm brings out the vegetables' flavor, softening them slightly and making them even juicier than they started out. It also makes the feta cheese very creamy.

If you do have leftovers, they will make a marvelous light lunch the next day, though you might want to pop the couscous into the microwave for just a few seconds to make everything nice and supple, especially if you've stored it in the fridge.

serves 6

1 large garlic clove, minced

¾ teaspoon plus 1 pinch kosher salt

2 teaspoons freshly squeezed lemon juice

¼ teaspoon freshly ground black pepper

3 tablespoons extra-virgin olive oil

1½ cups Israeli couscous, preferably whole wheat

1 cup fresh corn kernels (from 1 large ear)

1 large ripe tomato, diced

3 ounces feta cheese, crumbled (optional)

2 tablespoons chopped fresh basil

1. On a cutting board, use the flat side of a knife to mash together the garlic and a pinch of salt until a paste forms (or use a mortar and pestle). In a small bowl, whisk together the garlic paste, lemon juice, remaining ¾ teaspoon salt, and the pepper. Whisk in the oil.

2. Cook the couscous according to the package instructions; add the corn for the last 5 minutes of cooking. Drain well.

3. In a large bowl, combine the hot couscous-corn mixture, tomato, and vinaigrette. Let the couscous cool for about 10 minutes before gently folding in the feta (if using) and basil.

Shaved zucchini and avocado salad with green goddess dressing

I was a green goddess once, sort of. It was in high school, where I had a very brief solo in the school play. I cannot for the life of me remember what that play was, but my part involved me singing a little song while wearing a sea green toga and gold slippers in the latest goddess fashion.

If it weren't for the fact that I happen to love the creamy, anchovy saltiness of green goddess salad dressing, I probably wouldn't have even remembered this fifteen seconds of teenage fame. But now every time I whip up a batch of the herb-flecked emulsion, my mind flits over to those bright lights, briefly cringing at the memory before concentrating on the yumminess in front of me.

And this green goddess dressing is extremely good, a classic that I don't muck with very much. I've just tweaked the herb varieties and quantities to my liking, combining a lot of pungent parsley with a bit of cilantro and basil. I also use buttermilk as the base, which gives the dressing a lighter texture compared to the sour cream– and mayonnaise-laden versions you often see.

Green goddess dressing tastes good on almost any kind of vegetable matter (and fish, too); here I drizzle it all over thinly sliced ribbons of zucchini and chunks of velvety avocado. It's the sort of thing I'll make when it's so hot out that all the greens at the farmers' market look wilted and sad, but the zucchini are small, taut, and shining, just waiting to be lunch.

serves 4

FOR THE GREEN GODDESS DRESSING

½ cup plus 2 tablespoons packed fresh basil leaves

½ cup buttermilk

⅓ cup packed fresh parsley leaves

¼ cup packed fresh cilantro leaves

3 tablespoons olive oil

2 scallions, white and light green parts, sliced

1 anchovy fillet

1 small garlic clove, finely chopped

2½ teaspoons freshly squeezed lemon juice

¼ teaspoon kosher salt, plus more to taste

Freshly ground black pepper, to taste

1 medium zucchini or summer squash (about 8 ounces)

1 avocado, pitted, peeled, and cut into chunks

(continued)

Raw kale salad with anchovy-date dressing

A few years ago I made a raw kale salad, a recipe I adapted from Franny's restaurant in Brooklyn and subsequently published in my column in the *New York Times*.

Filled with tangy pecorino, loads of pungent garlic, and salty crisp bread crumbs, it became one of my favorite things in the world to eat—and I ate it as often as I could.

The great thing about the kale salad is it's ideal for entertaining. I could make it in advance and it would hold up during the whole party, wilting a little but getting tastier as it sat. The only thing I didn't like was that my husband, Daniel, who doesn't eat cheese, couldn't partake.

One day, while making a Daniel-friendly date-citrus-anchovy dressing to toss with arugula for a friend's party, I got the idea to use kale.

The slightly sticky, pungent date dressing was delicious, but it always wilted the arugula minutes after being dressed. Kale, however, would stand up to the dressing, and the whole thing seemed like it would be a nice, cheeseless alternative to my usual mix.

It worked beautifully, with the sweetness of the dates and salty, funky tang of the anchovies mitigating the assertive, green flavor of the kale. The salad was wonderful from the moment it graced the table, and then proceeded to get better as the evening wore on, softening, deepening, and becoming even more interesting and complex with the passing hours—the perfect guest at any party.

serves 6

6 to 8 large Medjool dates, pitted, smashed, and finely chopped

6 anchovy fillets, finely chopped

3 garlic cloves, finely chopped

Finely grated zest of 2 oranges

Finely grated zest of 2 lemons

½ cup extra-virgin olive oil

1 tablespoon plus 1 teaspoon red wine vinegar, plus more to taste

2 large or 3 small bunches Tuscan kale, stems removed

Coarse sea salt, for serving

1. In a medium bowl, stir together the dates (use more dates if you like a sweeter salad and fewer if you prefer a less sweet salad), anchovies, garlic, orange zest, and lemon zest. Stir in the olive oil and vinegar.

2. Wash and dry the kale leaves; stack the leaves and slice them thinly crosswise. Transfer the greens to a large salad bowl. Add the vinaigrette and toss gently to combine. Add salt and more vinegar, if needed.

Cumin seed roasted cauliflower with salted yogurt, mint, and pomegranate seeds

When the nights turn blustery and the temperature drops, I know that roasted vegetable season has arrived, and I embrace it with reckless abandon. I'll roast any kind of sturdy vegetable that I can cut up and fit into my oven, but one of my favorites is cauliflower, preferably tossed with cumin seeds. Not only does the cumin act as a natural remedy to help reduce the dreaded intestinal gas factor (or so I've been told), but it also adds a pleasant earthy flavor to balance the assertive tang of the vegetable.

Roasted cauliflower with cumin makes a nice and simple side dish. Even Dahlia will eat it if she's distracted enough. But recently I made it into lunch. I roasted up a small head all for myself, and added a topping of salted yogurt (which is simply a good full-fat yogurt with a little kosher salt mixed in), a few leftover pomegranate seeds (which I can buy at my local market already picked out of the husk), and a smattering of bright green chopped fresh mint. It was a perfect light lunch. It could even be dinner, served over brown rice, bulgur, or some other filling, toasty grain, for a warming meal to start out roasting season right.

serves 2

1 large head cauliflower, cut into bite-size florets

2 tablespoons extra-virgin olive oil

1 teaspoon cumin seeds

½ teaspoon kosher salt, plus more as needed

½ teaspoon freshly ground black pepper

Plain full-fat yogurt, for serving

Chopped fresh mint leaves, for serving

Pomegranate seeds, for serving

1. Preheat the oven to 425°F.

2. Toss the cauliflower with the oil, cumin seeds, salt, and pepper. Spread the mixture in an even layer on a large baking sheet. Roast, tossing occasionally, until the cauliflower is tender and its edges are toasty, 20 to 30 minutes.

3. Whisk a pinch of salt into the yogurt. Dollop the yogurt on top of the cauliflower and strew the mint and pomegranate seeds over the yogurt.

Sesame soba salad with roasted shiitakes and tofu croutons

For most of my life, I ate buckwheat one way—as kasha at my grandmother's table. She served it in the traditional Russian Jewish style, boiled until just shy of mushy, then topped with sweet, charred, near-black onions and plenty of sautéed mushrooms.

Then I went to college and discovered a whole other buckwheat culture bobbing away in the soup pots of the Upper West Side's Japanese restaurants. Smooth, gentle soba noodles immediately replaced nubby kasha as my favorite buckwheat endeavor, and they still are. I just love how the smoky earthiness of the grain is softened by the silky, slippery texture of the noodles, which slide past my lips when slicked with broth or oil (in this case, fragrant, toasty sesame oil).

This robust and sustaining soba salad, seasoned with ginger, orange juice, and soy sauce and garnished with crunchy cucumber, is an ideal dish to serve to all your gluten-free vegetarian friends, of which I have at least one. Just make sure you buy gluten-free soy sauce or tamari, and certified gluten-free soba noodles, because although pure buckwheat is naturally gluten free (despite the name, buckwheat is a grass, not a grain), soba noodles are sometimes made with regular wheat flour.

serves 4

FOR THE SALAD

7 to 8 ounces shiitake mushrooms, stems removed

2 tablespoons toasted (Asian) sesame oil, plus more to taste

3½ tablespoons soy sauce, plus more to taste

Pinch kosher salt

½ (12.8-ounce) package soba noodles (see headnote)

1½ tablespoons freshly squeezed orange juice (from about ½ small orange)

1 tablespoon rice vinegar

1 tablespoon grated peeled fresh ginger

1 medium cucumber, peeled

2 scallions, thinly sliced

2 tablespoons chopped fresh cilantro

1 tablespoon lightly toasted sesame seeds

FOR THE CROUTONS (OPTIONAL)

½ pound extra-firm tofu, drained and sliced into ¾-inch-thick slabs

1 tablespoon peanut oil or olive oil

2 tablespoons tamari or soy sauce

1½ teaspoons toasted (Asian) sesame oil

(continued)

1. MAKE THE SALAD: Preheat the oven to 400°F.

2. Slice the mushroom caps into ¼-inch-wide strips. Toss the mushrooms with 1 tablespoon of the sesame oil, ½ tablespoon of the soy sauce, and a pinch of salt. Spread the mushrooms in a single layer on a baking sheet. Roast, tossing occasionally, until the mushrooms are tender and slightly golden, 8 to 10 minutes.

3. Cook the soba noodles according to the package instructions. Drain and rinse quickly under cold running water; drain again completely.

4. In a bowl, whisk together the remaining 3 tablespoons soy sauce and 1 tablespoon sesame oil, the orange juice, vinegar, and ginger.

5. Cut the cucumber lengthwise into quarters and scoop out the seeds with a spoon. Cut each quarter crosswise into thin slices.

6. MAKE THE TOFU CROUTONS, IF DESIRED: Pat the tofu slabs dry with a paper towel. In a nonstick pan over medium heat, heat the peanut oil. When it shimmers, add the tofu and let it cook undisturbed (stand away from the tofu) for 3 minutes. It should be golden brown on the bottom. Flip the tofu pieces and cook for about 2 minutes more, until the underside is golden. In a small bowl, whisk together the tamari or soy sauce and sesame oil. Pour it into the pan with the croutons and cook for 1 minute more. Drain the croutons on a paper towel–lined plate.

7. ASSEMBLE THE SALAD: In a large bowl, toss together the noodles, cucumber, mushrooms, scallions, cilantro, sesame seeds, and dressing. Serve topped with tofu croutons, if desired. Drizzle the salad with more soy sauce and sesame oil just before serving if it needs perking up.

Sausage salad with radicchio and frisée

This is a take on a bitter greens salad with bacon vinaigrette; I've just substituted one pork product for another. The nice thing about the sausage is that it's unexpected and has a softer yet more complex bite than crunchy bacon. It's also more of a complete meal—either a light dinner or a hearty lunch. Good bread and butter, maybe drizzled with a little honey, are all you need alongside.

serves 2 to 4

1 large garlic clove

Pinch kosher salt, plus more to taste

½ pound Italian sausage, casings removed

1 tablespoon extra-virgin olive oil, plus more to taste

1 tablespoon red wine vinegar

1 small head radicchio, halved, cored, and sliced

1 small head frisée, torn into pieces

1. On a cutting board, use the flat side of a knife to mash together the garlic and salt until a paste forms (or use a mortar and pestle).

2. In a skillet over medium-high heat, cook the sausage in the oil, stirring, until browned, about 5 minutes. Stir in the garlic paste and vinegar and cook, scraping up any browned bits from the bottom of the pan, until the garlic is fragrant, 1 to 2 minutes more.

3. Place the radicchio and frisée in a large bowl. Add the sausage mixture and pan drippings and toss well. Season with salt and olive oil to taste and serve immediately.

Frisée salad with bacon and eggs

In my pre-child, going-out-on-the-town days, I used to frequent the Odeon, back when it was one of the few late-night restaurants where you could get a full meal at one a.m. (now even typing this is making me tired). I'd pop in postdancing, ravenous, and order the frisée salad, which was composed of a shower of plump confited garlic cloves, a pig's worth of fried lardons, plenty of crunchy croutons, and a mound of blue cheese. Somewhere in the bowl were a few wilted frisée leaves, though to be honest I might have left them on the bottom of the bowl. This salad was not about dieting. It was about flavorful excess, and I adored it.

Fast-forward to my more restrained, grown-up version. I have since discovered that I actually like frisée, and so in my salad, I use enough of the pale, curly greens to actually contribute some wholesome vegetable matter to the mix. I skipped the caramelized garlic confit because this is a spontaneous salad and I never seem to have jars full of garlic confit around when I want them. Instead, I go the more pungent route and paste up a garlic clove to add to the dressing. If you don't feel like going to the trouble of poaching the eggs, go ahead and fry them instead. The blue cheese is strictly optional. If Daniel is supping with me, I leave it out. But if I'm alone, I pile it on and flash back to those crazy, underage dancing days—from the sedentary comfort of my couch.

serves 2 as a light main course, 4 as an appetizer

4 strips bacon (6 ounces)	2 tablespoons extra-virgin olive oil
1 large garlic clove, finely chopped	4 large eggs
¼ teaspoon plus 1 pinch kosher salt	8 ounces frisée
1 teaspoon red wine vinegar	2 scallions, thinly sliced
1 teaspoon Dijon mustard	2 ounces blue cheese, crumbled (about ½ cup)

1. In a hot skillet over medium-high heat, fry the bacon until crisp. Transfer to a paper towel–lined plate to drain. Let cool slightly; crumble.

2. On a cutting board, use the flat side of a knife to mash together the garlic and a pinch of salt until a paste forms (or use a mortar and pestle). In a small bowl, whisk together the garlic paste, vinegar, mustard, and remaining ¼ teaspoon salt. Slowly whisk in the oil until it is incorporated.

3. Fill a medium pot three-quarters full with water; bring to a simmer. Crack the eggs, one at a time, into a ramekin. Lower the ramekin to the surface of the water and let the egg slide into it. Use a spoon to gently nudge the white closer to the yolk as it simmers. Cook until the white is just set, about 2 minutes for soft-poached eggs. Remove each egg with a slotted spoon and set them aside on a plate while you cook the remainder.

4. In a large bowl, toss together the frisée, crumbled bacon, scallions, and dressing. Divide the salad among individual serving plates. Top each with a poached egg and a sprinkle of crumbled cheese.

Queso fresco quesadillas with papaya-avocado salsa

Before I had a child of my own, one of the best reasons to visit my friends with toddling children was as an excuse to eat grilled cheese sandwiches.

Sure, I treasured the youngster rituals of dumping everything out of Aunty Melissa's purse, watching out the window for passing construction vehicles ("Look, Elliot! Cement mixer!"), and playing dress-up and hide-and-seek. But just as much, I love lunchtime, when almost every mother I know asks: "Who wants grilled cheese?" The loudest "yes" is unfailingly mine.

These days, I'm often called upon to make lunch for small children and their ravenous parents. And that's when I turn to something cheesy, gooey, yet a bit more adult. Something that would not only please both the kids and adults but also pair well with cocktails.

The answer is quesadillas: soft tortillas filled with mild cheese, then broiled until crispy and molten-centered. The kids gobble them up in their plainest incarnation. And on the side, adults can dunk them in a bracing papaya and avocado salsa. Everyone is always delighted.

serves 2

FOR THE SALSA

1 cup cubed fresh papaya

½ avocado, pitted, peeled, and cubed

¼ cup cubed seeded cucumber

3 tablespoons chopped fresh cilantro

2 tablespoons finely chopped red onion

2 tablespoons freshly squeezed orange juice

2 tablespoons freshly squeezed lime juice

1 tablespoon extra-virgin olive oil

½ teaspoon honey, or to taste

½ teaspoon kosher salt

Freshly ground black pepper, to taste

4 (6-inch) corn tortillas

4 ounces queso fresco

1. Preheat the broiler and place an oven rack 4 inches from the heat.

2. MAKE THE SALSA: In a bowl, stir together the salsa ingredients. Taste and adjust the seasoning, if necessary.

3. Place 2 tortillas on a baking sheet. Crumble the queso fresco over the tortillas. Top with the remaining tortillas. Broil for 1 to 2 minutes per side, flipping once halfway through, until the cheese is melted and the tortillas are golden.

4. Quarter the quesadillas and top each section with 1 tablespoon of the salsa. Serve immediately.

Deviled egg salad with anchovies, hot smoked paprika, and tomato

Egg salad makes a convenient lunch if you are not transporting it anywhere in the summer. There are always eggs and mayonnaise in the fridge, and that's all you strictly need as long as you add copious grindings of black pepper to break up the eggy monotony.

But one day, I was in the mood to zip up my sandwich with various seasonings and condiments. My idea was to approach egg salad like deviled eggs, adding pungent dashes of this and that as I would to the yolk mixture before stuffing it back into its wobbly egg white boat.

I opened the fridge. There were the anchovies singing their little fishy siren song from their cylindrical glass jar. How could I resist?

I chopped them up and mixed them into the mayo, adding cider vinegar for brightness, garlic for oomph, and a little smoked paprika for heat and color (and because no deviled egg is complete without paprika). Then I layered the egg salad onto toasted bread. There were ripe tomatoes on the counter, and I sliced one up and nestled it over the eggs. It added the perfect juiciness—and a certain *je ne sais quoi*. Now I make my signature egg salad whenever the craving strikes, which is quite often, it turns out.

serves 2

3 tablespoons mayonnaise

2 anchovies, minced

½ teaspoon apple cider vinegar

Pinch hot smoked paprika

1 garlic clove, minced

Pinch kosher salt

2 large eggs, hard-cooked, peeled, and chopped

4 slices bread, toasted

1 ripe tomato, sliced

1. In a large bowl, mix together the mayonnaise, anchovies, vinegar, and paprika. On a cutting board, use the flat side of a knife to mash together the garlic and salt until a paste forms (or use a mortar and pestle). Add the garlic paste to the bowl and toss well to combine. Mix in the eggs.

2. Divide the salad between 2 slices of bread, top with tomato, and sandwich with the remaining 2 bread slices. Serve immediately.

Pan bagnat

There are plenty of ways to flatten a *pan bagnat*, the traditional tuna and vegetable sandwich from Nice.

You could weight it with some heavy books or one nice fat brick.

Or you could find a child of about seven and simply have her sit on it.

This was my parents' preferred method. Mimicking the cafes on the Côte d'Azur, my mother would slice a round crusty loaf in half; anoint it with oil, vinegar, and garlic; and stuff it with tuna and tomatoes. Then my sister and I would alternate sandwich-squashing shifts until the oil and vinegar inundated and "bathed" the well-wrapped loaf (*pan bagnat* translates to "bathed bread").

When I made the sandwich again recently, however, I didn't have a seven-year-old child to sit on it, so I filled the kettle and placed it on top of a baking pan to weight it down.

Twenty minutes later, the bread was still crusty on the outside, but perfumed with garlic, good olive oil, and the juice of sweet August tomatoes. The saline flavors of anchovy, tuna, mustard, and olives had unified into a delectably pungent whole, softened by the cucumber, egg, and some fresh basil leaves that I laid on top. Even without the sun, sand, and Mediterranean Sea, even without my parents and sister and cold bottles of Orangina, it still tasted just like I remembered, maybe even better.

serves 2 or 3

1 very small garlic clove, minced

1 teaspoon red wine vinegar

½ teaspoon Dijon mustard

Pinch salt

Pinch freshly ground black pepper

2 anchovy fillets, minced (optional)

2 tablespoons extra-virgin olive oil

1 (8-inch) round very crusty country loaf or small ciabatta, halved

½ Kirby cucumber, or ¼ regular cucumber (see Note)

1 ripe medium tomato, sliced

½ small red onion, sliced

1 (5- to 6-ounce) jar tuna in olive oil, drained

8 large fresh basil leaves

2 tablespoons sliced pitted olives (preferably a mix of black and green)

1 large egg, hard-cooked, peeled, and thinly sliced

1. In a small bowl, whisk together the garlic, vinegar, mustard, salt, pepper, and anchovies (if using). Slowly drizzle in the olive oil, whisking constantly.

(continued)

2. If using a country loaf, pull out some of the soft interior crumb to form a cavity. (If using a ciabatta, you won't need to eliminate anything.)

3. If using a Kirby cucumber, thinly slice it. If using a regular cucumber, peel it, halve it lengthwise, and scoop out the seeds from one half. Thinly slice half of the seedless half to give you a quarter of the original whole. Add the sliced cucumber to the vinaigrette and toss well.

4. Spread half the tomato slices on the bottom of the bread loaf. Top with half the cucumbers and some vinaigrette, then with the onion slices, tuna, basil leaves, olives, and egg slices. Top the egg with the remaining cucumbers, vinaigrette, and tomato slices. Cover with the top of the bread loaf and firmly press the sandwich together.

5. Wrap the sandwich tightly in foil, waxed paper, or plastic wrap, then place in a plastic bag. Put the sandwich under a weight such as a cast-iron skillet topped with a filled kettle, or have a small child about seven years old sit on the sandwich. Weight the sandwich for 7 to 10 minutes, then flip and weight it for 7 to 10 minutes more (or as long as you can get the child to sit still). Unwrap, slice, and serve immediately, or keep it wrapped for up to 8 hours before serving.

note: You can substitute seeded sliced green bell pepper for the cucumber.

A perfect tomato sandwich

Of all the seasonal produce about which I wax poetic in these pages, nothing gives me goose bumps like a ripe summer tomato.

Meaty and succulent, its velvety flesh enclosing a fragrant jelly of golden seeds and dripping with sweet pink juice, a summer tomato is everything its cold-weather counterpart isn't, including cheap and abundant.

Nothing, and I mean nothing, beats a good old tomato sandwich.

Tomato sandwiches and I go way back. I've always had a fondness for them ever since I read *Harriet the Spy* in third grade. Unlike Harriet, who likes hers on soft white bread for lunch every day, I like mine on toast to give it some crunch (and to stave off the soggy factor).

The recipe that follows makes a simple sandwich that doesn't seem like much on paper, but believe me, when made with a couple of bursting-with-juice heirloom tomatoes that have never seen a fridge; good, crusty, firm bread; creamery butter that tastes like sunshine; and a generous sprinkle of crunchy sea salt, it's about the most perfect thing a person could eat on a sultry August afternoon. Or morning. Or night. A tomato sandwich is wonderful anytime—anytime in tomato season, that is.

serves 1

2 slices crusty bread with a dense crumb

1 or 2 ripe tomatoes, depending on how big the tomatoes are, how hungry you are, and how large your bread slices are

At least 1 tablespoon good butter

Flaky sea salt and freshly ground black pepper, to taste

1. Toast the bread until crunchy and golden. While it's toasting, slice the tomatoes, taking out the brown core.

2. As soon as the toast is ready, spread it thickly with the butter. And I mean thickly, using at least a tablespoon and probably a lot more. I use about a tablespoon and a half, but then again, my bread slices are on the commodious side. If the butter isn't salted, sprinkle a little salt on top, then top with the tomatoes. You can overlap them or not, depending on how thickly you've sliced them.

3. Sprinkle the tomatoes with salt and grind on some black pepper. Eat with your hands. A knife and fork diminishes the tactile pleasure here.

Salami and horseradish Cheddar bagel sandwich

I recently had a grilled cheese craving strike when I was passing by my local bagel shop. Because cream cheese doesn't have the gooeyness factor of aged cheese and would simply ooze out in the pan if you tried to grill it, I bought a block of horseradish Cheddar along with my poppy seed bagel.

Back at home, waiting for the bagel to toast, I noshed on salami from the fridge, remembering an old friend who'd fry her salami before making it into a sandwich. I fried up a few slices and added them to my cheesy bagel along with rounds of red onion for crunch. Spicy, rich, and fatty, with a meaty edge from the salami, it was definitely as good as regular grilled cheese, and nearly as good as my regular bagel and lox.

serves 2

2 bagels, halved

3 ounces horseradish Cheddar cheese, sliced (or substitute horseradish Cheddar spread)

¼ pound salami, thinly sliced

½ small red onion, thinly sliced

1. In a toaster oven or in an oven preheated to 500°F, toast the bagel halves until pale golden. Top each with some of the cheese and continue toasting until the cheese begins to melt.

2. Meanwhile, in a skillet over medium heat, fry the salami slices until golden, about 3 minutes. Place the salami and red onion on the bottom bagel halves. Cover with the bagel tops and serve.

Crisp and juicy soft-shell crab sandwiches with caper berry tartar sauce

When my mother cooks crabs, she dips them in flour, fries them up until they're coral-hued and crisp, and serves them with lemon wedges and fresh herbs. For years I thought that was the only proper way to prepare soft-shell crabs. But one day my mind settled on something different—fried crab sandwiches. I wanted a docile starch to soak up all the saline crab juices, and toasted bread is an ideal vehicle.

My mental recipe was simple: Fry the crabs like my mother does, then slip them onto toast blanketed with homemade tartar sauce.

I had planned to use regular capers, which are traditional in tartar sauce, but while I was searching for them in the fridge, I came upon the caperberries. These are the plump, podlike fruit of the caper plant (capers are the buds). Soft in the mouth, caper berries are juicy and riddled with crunchy seeds. I chopped them up and mixed them into the sauce.

Then I fried up the crabs, their bellies puffing and edges crisping, and made them into sandwiches with lots of the tartar sauce and some arugula for freshness.

I sat down and took a bite. The first thing that hit me was a layered complexity of crunches—crab bits, toasted bread, and caperberry seeds jumbling in my mouth.

Then the crab liquor started to flow. The bread sopped up most of it, but some errant drops escaped down my chin. I just licked them up as fast as I could.

serves 2

FOR THE TARTAR SAUCE

1 garlic clove, finely minced

Pinch kosher salt, plus more to taste

2 teaspoons freshly squeezed lemon juice

2 tablespoons mayonnaise

2 tablespoons chopped onion

2 teaspoons chopped fresh soft herbs, such as basil, parsley, chives, tarragon, or fennel fronds

Freshly ground black pepper, to taste

1 to 2 teaspoons chopped caper berries, plus more to taste (see Note)

FOR THE SANDWICH

All-purpose flour, for dipping

Kosher salt and freshly ground black pepper, to taste

2 soft-shell crabs, cleaned if desired

2 to 3 tablespoons olive oil (enough to coat the bottom of the pan)

4 slices freshly toasted crusty country bread, or 2 ciabatta rolls, halved

Lettuce or arugula, for serving

Lemon wedges, for serving

(continued)

1. MAKE THE TARTAR SAUCE: On a cutting board, use the flat side of a knife to mash together the garlic and salt until a paste forms (or use a mortar and pestle). Scrape the paste into a small bowl and stir in the lemon juice. Stir well to help dissolve the salt. Stir in the remaining tartar sauce ingredients and season with more salt and pepper if you like.

2. Put some flour in a pie plate and season with salt and pepper. Dip the crabs into the seasoned flour, shaking off any excess. In a skillet over medium to high heat, heat the olive oil, then add the crabs and cook until they turn brown and crisp, about 2 minutes per side.

3. Slather 2 pieces of the bread with the tartar sauce and add the crabs and lettuce or arugula. Top with the remaining bread (you can slather it with tartar sauce, too, if you like). Serve with lemon wedges.

note: You can buy caper berries pickled in brine at specialty food shops. Or substitute regular capers, which you can leave whole.

dinners

Fresh corn polenta with roasted ratatouille and ricotta

Traditional ratatouille recipes call for sautéing all the elements—eggplant, zucchini, peppers, etc.—individually, then combining them at the end. The idea is that by keeping the vegetables separate, you respect their different cooking times (so each one is cooked until just soft but not falling apart) and maintain their integrity of flavor.

While I applaud this technique, I admit that I no longer follow it. It's just too darn labor-intensive, especially for summertime. Instead, I roast everything in the oven all at once, which browns the vegetables and condenses their flavors, adding a caramel note that's absent in more classically stewed ratatouilles.

The downside is that roasting will heat up your kitchen more than stovetop cooking. But since you don't have to babysit each type of vegetable in the skillet at a time, you can retire to the air-conditioned living room while it does.

When the vegetables are bronzed and glistening and slack in the pan, I toss them with some sweet roasted garlic and a few drops of lemon juice, if the caramelized flavors seem a bit cloying.

This roasted ratatouille needs nothing but a fork and plate to make it a completely satisfying culinary experience (even the plate is optional if you're the one holding the bowl). But something starchy—pasta, couscous, or soft polenta studded with fresh corn kernels—raises the dish to celestial heights.

serves 2 as a main dish, 4 as a side

2 small eggplant (about ¾ pound), cut into 1-inch chunks

2 small zucchini (about ½ pound), cut into 1-inch chunks

2 small red bell peppers (about ½ pound), cut into 1-inch chunks

2 large fresh rosemary sprigs

¼ cup plus 1 teaspoon extra-virgin olive oil

Kosher salt and freshly ground black pepper, to taste

1 pint cherry tomatoes

2 garlic cloves, unpeeled

Freshly squeezed lemon juice, to taste (optional)

FOR THE POLENTA

1 bay leaf

¾ teaspoon fine sea salt

1 cup polenta or coarse cornmeal

1½ cups fresh corn kernels (from 2 small ears)

Fresh ricotta cheese, for serving

Torn fresh basil leaves, for serving (optional)

(continued)

1. In a food processor fitted with a fine grating attachment, shred the squash. (Or use a box grater, but it will be harder to do. You could also just cut it into small cubes; it won't dissolve into a sauce but will be differently pleasing.) In a small saucepan, bring the broth to a simmer. Melt the butter in a large skillet over medium heat. Add the leek and cook, stirring occasionally, until soft, 5 to 7 minutes. Stir in the garlic and cook it until fragrant, about 1 minute. Add the rice, squash, rosemary, and salt. Stir until most of the grains of rice appear semitranslucent, 3 to 4 minutes. This means they have absorbed some of the fat from the pan, which will help keep the grains separate from each other as they form their creamy sauce.

2. Pour the wine into the pan and let it cook off for about 2 minutes. Add a ladleful of broth (about ½ cup) and cook, stirring it constantly and making sure to scrape around the sides, until most of the liquid has evaporated. Continue adding broth, a ladleful at a time, and stirring almost constantly until the risotto has turned creamy and thick, and the grains of rice are tender with a bit of bite, 25 to 30 minutes (you may not need all the stock). Pluck out the rosemary and stir in the lemon zest, lemon juice, and black pepper. Taste and add more salt and lemon juice if needed. Garnish with the pistachios and optional cheese before serving.

Spicy black beans with chorizo and jalapeños

My college friend Mara turned me on to this dish, which she made in her dorm room on a weekly basis. Her version was minimalist. She'd warm up a can of Goya black beans, stirring a little ground cumin and oregano into the pot. Then she'd pour it over cooked rice and top it with fried eggs and hot sauce. It was satisfying, cheap, and easy enough to make while simultaneously trying to memorize the minutia of the biliary tract.

My recipe is slightly more involved. I add sautéed vegetables because I love the gentle crunch of peppers and onions amid all that carbohydrate goodness of beans and rice. The optional chorizo adds spice and meatiness to what is otherwise one of the heartier of vegetarian entrées. Best of all, it's still satisfying, cheap, and easy enough to make while wrangling a toddler underfoot—which may or may not be easier than collegiate-level biology.

serves 2

2 tablespoons extra-virgin olive oil

3 ounces cured chorizo, cut into ½-inch cubes (optional)

1 Vidalia or other sweet onion, diced

2 large garlic cloves, finely chopped

1 red bell pepper, diced

1 jalapeño, seeded and finely chopped

¾ teaspoon dried oregano

¾ teaspoon ground cumin

1 (15.5-ounce) can black beans, drained but not rinsed (or substitute 1¾ cups freshly cooked black beans)

¾ teaspoon kosher salt

3 tablespoons chopped fresh cilantro

Hot sauce, to taste

Cooked brown or white rice, for serving

2 large fried eggs, for serving (optional)

1. In a large skillet over medium-high heat, warm the oil. Add the chorizo and cook until light golden, about 3 minutes. Stir in the onion, garlic, bell pepper, and jalapeño. Cook, stirring, until the vegetables are softened, about 7 minutes. Stir in the oregano and cumin; cook for 1 minute more. Stir in the beans and salt and simmer gently for 5 minutes.

2. Remove the pot from the heat. Stir in the cilantro and hot sauce to taste. Serve over rice. Top each plate with a fried egg, if desired.

Carroty mac and cheese

Like most little kids, Dahlia loves macaroni and cheese, and I've made it for her in many guises, running the gamut of techniques. My aim is always the same—to make the dish quickly with a minimum amount of effort and to use a maximum of vegetables that she will tolerate and not pick out.

This is one of both our favorites. It's comforting, crusty topped, soft centered, and very cheesy—but not at all sophisticated. Just simple homemade food with the added grown-up appeal of lots of healthful carrots tossed into the mix. It's a huge hit with the under-three crowd and their parents, too.

It's a straightforward recipe that comes together without much fuss, other than having to grate some carrots. But to make up for that, I've eliminated the need to make a cheese sauce on the top of the stove. Instead, I toss the hot pasta with grated Cheddar, butter, sour cream for creaminess, and eggs to hold it all together. The grated carrots get boiled along with the pasta, so cooking them isn't an extra step. And the tiny orange shreds look so much like the Cheddar that your kids might not even notice them. Dahlia certainly hasn't, and while I've never lied to her about their inclusion, I might have left out the word *carrot* in the dish description—accidentally, of course.

serves 6

1 teaspoon kosher salt, plus more for the pasta water

2 cups whole wheat macaroni

2½ cups coarsely grated carrots (about 8 small)

3 cups grated sharp Cheddar cheese

4 tablespoons (½ stick) unsalted butter, cut into pieces

¾ cup sour cream

¼ cup whole milk

2 large eggs

¾ teaspoon mustard powder

¼ teaspoon freshly ground black pepper

¼ cup finely grated Parmesan cheese

1. Preheat the oven to 400°F. Arrange a rack in the top third of the oven. Grease an 8-inch-square baking pan. Bring a large pot of salted water to a boil.

2. Cook the macaroni in the boiling water according to the package instructions. Add the carrots 3 minutes before the pasta is finished cooking; drain well and return to the pot.

(continued)

3. While the pasta is still hot, stir in 2½ cups of the Cheddar and the butter. In a bowl, whisk together the sour cream, milk, eggs, salt, mustard powder, and pepper. Fold the mixture into the pasta.

4. Scrape the mixture into the prepared pan. Sprinkle the remaining ½ cup Cheddar and the Parmesan over the top. Bake until the casserole is firm to the touch and golden brown, about 30 minutes.

Farro pasta with spicy salami tomato sauce and fresh mint

This is what Daniel ate the night before he ran his second New York City marathon.

For a premarathon meal, my instinct would have been to cook up simple white pasta, but Daniel asked for whole grains. It might not be as efficient a carb to digest, but it would stay with him longer, he said, which was a plus.

I was able to score some really good, nutty farro pasta at my local gourmet market. Whole wheat would have worked nicely, too, but I like the slightly more rustic texture and earthier flavor of the farro stuff.

I knew it would be best served topped with a hearty, spicy, assertively flavored sauce that would stand up to its full flavor. I made a sauce inspired by Franny's, my neighborhood Italian restaurant. There, Andrew Feinberg, the chef (and my friend), makes a fiery salami pasta rich with plum tomatoes and good, herby olive oil. For his version, he makes his own extra-spicy sopressata for the sauce. I used regular spicy sopressata fired up with a good pinch of crushed red pepper flakes.

Andrew tops his pasta with plenty of grated cheese, but I left it off and added some chopped fresh mint instead.

Daniel and I gobbled it up, and it gave him the energy he needed to rock the race and me enough to cheer him on from the sidelines in the most energetic fashion I could muster.

serves 4

FOR THE TOMATO SAUCE
(MAKES ABOUT 2 CUPS)

¼ cup extra-virgin olive oil

½ yellow onion, chopped

1 garlic clove, thinly sliced

½ teaspoon kosher salt, plus more to taste

Pinch freshly ground black pepper, plus more to taste

1 (28-ounce) can San Marzano tomatoes

FOR THE PASTA

Kosher salt, to taste

1 pound farro pasta or whole wheat pasta of a short thick shape, such as penne

½ pound spicy sopressata, casing removed

2 tablespoons extra-virgin olive oil, plus more for serving

½ teaspoon crushed red pepper flakes

Chopped fresh mint, for garnish

(continued)

1. MAKE THE TOMATO SAUCE: In a medium saucepan over medium-low heat, heat the oil. Add the onion, garlic, salt, and pepper. Cook, covered, until the vegetables are very soft, 5 to 7 minutes. Pour in the tomatoes and their liquid. Simmer until the sauce thickens and the oil separates and rises to the surface of the sauce, about 25 minutes. Run the sauce through a food mill fitted with the large disc; season with additional salt and pepper.

2. MAKE THE PASTA: Bring a large pot of heavily salted water to a boil. Cook the pasta until very al dente (remove it about 2 minutes before the time indicated on the package for al dente). Drain the pasta well.

3. Cut the sopressata into batons about 2 inches long and ¼ inch thick.

4. In a large, straight-sided skillet over medium-high heat, heat the oil. Add the sopressata and cook, stirring occasionally, until the sausage is light golden and has rendered some of its fat. Pour in the tomato sauce and red pepper flakes. Cook over high heat until the sauce looks dry and turns golden around the edges, about 8 minutes.

5. Remove the sauce from the heat and stir in ¼ cup water. Add the pasta. Return the skillet to the heat and cook, tossing occasionally, until the sauce reduces and tightens around the pasta, 2 to 3 minutes.

6. Divide the pasta among individual serving plates. Drizzle each plate with olive oil, sprinkle with mint, and serve.

Pasta with Turkish-style lamb, eggplant, and yogurt sauce

When Turkish culinary historian Engin Akin taught me how to make *manti*—hand-formed lamb dumplings—on a trip to Istanbul, every step was exquisitely and most labor-intensively wrought.

Once cooked, the *manti* was coated with thick yogurt and plenty of melted brown butter seasoned with ground chile. Ever since, I've dreamed of making platters of buttery *manti* at home, but I needed a way to shorten the process without compromising that savory, near-sacred combination of butter, lamb, garlic, yogurt, and more butter.

I did some online research, and saw that *manti*-loving bloggers routinely substituted dried pasta for handmade dough, topping it with sautéed ground lamb and yogurt. It seemed like as good a place as any to start.

At home, I tossed eggplant cubes in oil and put them in the oven for a possible side dish. While the pasta boiled, I sautéed the lamb with garlic and shallots, seasoning it with fresh mint.

When I drained the pasta and tossed it with the lamb, I realized I could have used twice as much lamb, but it was too late for that. To compensate, I folded in the roasted eggplant. Then I added thick Greek yogurt spiked with pungent fresh garlic, and, as per my memory of Ms. Akin's feast, much more of the red pepper–spiced browned butter than I knew was good for me. As with the *manti*, butter and yogurt melded into a rich sauce, generously gilding the lamb, pasta, and, in this case, eggplant with garlicky abandon. So much for leftovers the next day.

serves 2 or 3

½ teaspoon kosher or coarse sea salt, plus more as needed

1 large eggplant (about 1 pound), cut into ½-inch cubes

5 tablespoons extra-virgin olive oil

3 fat garlic cloves, minced

1 large shallot, minced

1 pound ground lamb

¼ teaspoon red pepper flakes, preferably Urfa or Aleppo (see Note), plus more to taste

Freshly ground black pepper, to taste

1½ tablespoons chopped fresh mint or dill, plus more to taste

½ pound bow-tie or other pasta

6 tablespoons (¾ stick) unsalted butter

⅔ cup plain Greek yogurt

(continued)

1. Preheat the oven to 450°F. Bring a large pot of salted water to a boil for the pasta.

2. Toss the eggplant with 4 tablespoons of the oil and a large pinch of salt. Spread on a baking sheet, making sure there is room between the pieces, and roast until crisp and brown, 15 to 20 minutes. Check often to prevent burning.

3. In a large skillet over medium-high heat, heat the remaining 1 tablespoon oil. Add 2 minced garlic cloves and the shallot and sauté until fragrant, 1 to 2 minutes. Add the lamb, salt, red pepper flakes, and black pepper to taste and sauté until the lamb is no longer pink, about 5 minutes. Stir in the mint or dill and cook for 2 minutes more. Stir the eggplant into the lamb. Taste and adjust the seasonings.

4. Cook the pasta in the boiling water according to the package directions. Meanwhile, in a small saucepan, melt the butter. Cook until it turns golden brown and smells nutty, about 5 minutes. In a small bowl, stir together the yogurt, remaining minced garlic clove, and a pinch of salt.

5. Drain the pasta and spread on a serving platter. Top with the lamb-eggplant mixture, then with the yogurt sauce. Pour the melted butter over the top and sprinkle on additional red pepper flakes and mint or dill. Serve immediately.

note: You can buy Urfa (Turkish) or Aleppo (Syrian) pepper flakes at specialty markets or online at www.kalustyans.com. Or substitute a mild ground chile powder. Do not use crushed red pepper flakes; they will be too hot for this dish.

Whole wheat pizza with the very first cherry tomatoes, olives, and tuna

I learned how to make pizza from Andrew Feinberg of Franny's in Brooklyn, when I was assigned to write a series of articles about him for a now defunct *New York Times* Dining Section column called "The Chef."

His is arguably some of the best pizza in a city full of great pizza—with a slow-rising crust that is bubbly, singed in all the right spots, full of aromatic yeasty flavor, and shatteringly crisp.

The best part, for home cooks, is that you really can make a version of this fantastic pizza at home. Andrew and I came up with a technique of baking, then broiling the pizzas, which is surprisingly successful in a normal home range. Sure, in Andrew's 800°F wood-fired oven, the pizzas cook in about two minutes. At home, it takes about six. But the charred, crackling crusts are very similar in texture and flavor.

This is my version of Andrew's pie. I use a little whole wheat flour (25 percent, to be exact) in the crust, just to bump up the fiber content and give the crust a deeper, nuttier flavor. And yes, you really do have to refrigerate this dough overnight; the long, slow rise helps develop its yeasty, full flavor. The results are so good that we make pizza at home at least a few times a month, even though Franny's is only two blocks from our house. Andrew's pizza might be better at the restaurant, but at home we never have to wait for a table. And that counts for a lot.

makes 3 (12-inch) pizzas; serves 3 or 4

FOR THE DOUGH

1⅛ teaspoons active dry yeast
(half a ¼-ounce packet)

1 tablespoon plus 1 teaspoon
kosher salt

3 cups all-purpose flour, plus more
for dusting

1 cup whole wheat flour

Olive oil, for coating the bowl

FOR THE PIZZAS

6 garlic cloves, thinly sliced

Dried oregano, for sprinkling

Crushed red pepper flakes, for
sprinkling

1 cup good-quality tuna in olive oil,
drained and flaked

18 cherry tomatoes, halved

6 tablespoons pitted kalamata
olives, halved lengthwise

Olive oil, for drizzling

Coarse sea salt, for sprinkling

3 tablespoons thinly sliced
fresh basil

(continued)

1. MAKE THE DOUGH: Combine the yeast and 1¼ cups warm water in the bowl of an electric mixer fitted with the paddle attachment. Let the mixture sit until foamy, about 5 minutes. Add the salt and both flours. Mix on medium-high speed until the dough comes together, adding more warm water as needed. You should not knead the dough, but do mix until the dough just becomes supple and smooth. Place the dough in an oil-coated bowl and cover loosely with plastic wrap. Transfer to the refrigerator and let rise for at least 24 hours and up to 3 days.

2. When ready to use the dough, divide it into 3 equal-size pieces. Shape each piece into a ball. Let sit at room temperature for at least 30 minutes; this makes a big difference in the ease with which your dough will stretch to pizza-worthy size.

3. MAKE THE PIZZAS: Preheat the oven to 500°F. Arrange an oven rack in the top third of the oven. Place a pizza stone on the rack and let it heat for 1 hour. (Or use an overturned baking dish and preheat for 30 minutes.)

4. Turn a large baking sheet upside down and dust the surface with flour. Place a dough ball on a clean, lightly floured surface; dust the top of the dough with additional flour. Use your fingertips to flatten the dough into a round. Holding the dough in front of you like a steering wheel (with your hands at 10 o'clock and 2 o'clock), rotate the dough several times between your hands, stretching it slightly as you do so. Try to maintain as even a thickness as possible, with the outermost edges of the dough slightly thicker. Continue, working carefully around thin patches of dough to ensure that it does not tear, until you have a 12ish-inch round. (Or use a rolling pin to roll out the dough.)

5. Carefully set the dough down upon the floured baking sheet. Patch any tears or holes in the dough. Working quickly, scatter the dough with a third of the sliced garlic, a pinch of dried oregano, and a pinch of red pepper flakes. Scatter on a third of the tuna, 12 tomato halves, and 2 tablespoons olives.

6. Jiggle the pizza gently to make sure it is not sticking. Slide the pizza directly onto the hot stone; make sure to start holding the pan at the stone's back end so the entire pizza will fit. Drizzle the pizza generously with oil.

7. Bake the pizza until the underside is golden and the top is firm, 3 minutes. Turn off the oven and turn on the broiler. Broil the pizza until golden, crisp, and a bit blistery and charred in places, 1 to 4 minutes (watch it carefully to see that it does not burn). (If you have one of those ovens with the broiler in a separate drawer on the bottom, don't use the broiling method. Just leave the pizza in the 500°F oven until it is crisp and golden brown all over. It will take 8 to 15 minutes.) Remove the pizza from the oven and return the oven temperature to 500°F.

8. Use tongs to slide the pizza onto a large platter. Drizzle with oil and sprinkle with salt; garnish with basil. Repeat the process with the remaining dough balls and toppings.

Roasted shrimp and broccoli

When cooking seasonally, it's not just the ingredients that follow the weather. Techniques do, too.

In warmer months I'll savor broccoli raw in salads or steam it lightly to accentuate its grassy green flavor. But in winter, I want broccoli slow cooked, caramelized, and thoroughly soft. Roasting gets me there with a minimum of fuss.

I've served roasted broccoli florets, strewn with coriander and cumin seeds and maybe a pinch of chili powder, as finger food at fancy parties. I've eaten heaps of it for supper with nothing more than some bread and cheese on the side. I've pureed it into soup thinned down with chicken broth.

But one evening, I was itching to try something a little different, and wanted to add a quick-cooking protein I could roast along with the broccoli, preferably in the same pan.

Plump pink shrimp required no advance preparation, and the color would be gorgeous with the broccoli.

Having roasted shrimp on their own before, I knew their cooking time would be about half that of the broccoli, especially if I wanted supple florets.

So I slicked the broccoli with oil and seasonings and set it to roast. Ten minutes later, I tossed in the shrimp. After twenty minutes altogether, I ended up with juicy, meaty shrimp tinged with lemon zest, and spice-infused, tender, golden-edged broccoli. Perhaps best of all, there was only one dirty pan; easy cleanup is welcome in any season.

serves 4

2 pounds broccoli, cut into bite-size florets

4 tablespoons extra-virgin olive oil

1 teaspoon coriander seeds

1 teaspoon cumin seeds

1½ teaspoons kosher salt

1 teaspoon freshly ground black pepper

⅛ teaspoon hot chili powder

1 pound large shrimp, peeled and deveined

1¼ teaspoons finely grated lemon zest (from 1 large lemon)

Lemon wedges, for serving

1. Preheat the oven to 425°F.

2. In a large bowl, toss the broccoli with 2 tablespoons of the oil, the coriander, cumin, 1 teaspoon of the salt, ½ teaspoon of the pepper, and the chili powder. In a separate bowl, combine the shrimp, remaining 2 tablespoons oil, lemon zest, and remaining ½ teaspoon salt and ½ teaspoon pepper.

3. Spread the broccoli in a single layer on a baking sheet. Roast for 10 minutes. Add the shrimp to the baking sheet and toss with the broccoli. Roast, tossing once halfway through, until the shrimp are just opaque and the broccoli is tender and golden around the edges, about 10 minutes more. Serve with lemon wedges, or squeeze the lemon juice all over the shrimp and broccoli just before serving.

Sautéed scallops with tomatoes and preserved lemon

For years, Daniel and I harbored a small jar with one homemade preserved lemon bobbing along in it. Because Daniel had made it himself, we had neither the heart to eat it (it was the last one) nor throw it out.

Of course the minute after I finally did toss it out in a flurry of obsessive fridge cleaning, I regretted it. Preserved lemons, if you actually use them, can be a culinary treasure. They are one of those secret seasonings that makes everything you use them in taste better—brighter, more intense, and more aromatic.

So I bought a new jar. Then, as soon as I got home, I immediately pureed those cute, whole little lemons (taking out the seeds first) in the food processor and covered them with a bit of olive oil. That way whenever I wanted a little of that musky, zesty, earthy complexity that preserved lemons bring, I could just spoon some out and drop it into the pan or bowl or plate without having to stop and chop (though you could mince it up as needed if you like).

In this buoyant, tangy scallop dish, I added a dollop of the salty yellow paste to a pan of buttery scallops and chopped juicy tomato. The lemon brightened the flavors and added that extra-special layer of fermented flavor that plain citrus fruit just doesn't have. Served with noodles or couscous to soak up the buttery sauce, this recipe was about as simple as can be—instant gratification that took several years to puzzle out.

serves 2

1½ tablespoons unsalted butter

2 garlic cloves, finely chopped

1 pound sea scallops, patted dry

1 medium tomato, cored and chopped

1 tablespoon finely chopped or pureed preserved lemon

Kosher salt and freshly ground black pepper, to taste

In a large skillet over medium heat, melt the butter. Add the garlic and cook, stirring, until fragrant, about 1 minute. Add the scallops, tomato, lemon, and a pinch of salt. Cook, stirring, until the scallops are just opaque, about 2 minutes. Season with additional salt, if needed, and pepper. Serve over pasta, if desired.

Buttery, garlicky, spicy calamari with Israeli couscous

When I think of fast food, I think of calamari. It's probably one of the least expensive, tastiest, quickest-cooking sea creatures out there, all the while being sustainable and plentiful, so there's no reason not to eat it all the time. Which we do.

The squid I buy at the fish store is a snap to cook with because it comes well cleaned. I slice up the bodies while the oil heats, and this dish is ready in under 10 minutes.

The squid from the farmers' market, however, demands a bit more attention, since it comes straight off the fishing boat and can be sandy. I give it a strong rinse under lots of cold water to dislodge lingering grit (make sure to flush out the cavity). The clean, ocean flavor of this über-fresh squid makes it worth the extra sand-removal effort.

Once you've got your squid in order, this dish really does cook in minutes, so make sure you have everything else on the table—the salad in the bowl waiting to be tossed with vinaigrette, the wine poured, and the candles lit (yes, this dish is candle-worthy)—before you starting heating the pan. In minutes, you'll serve a savory, garlicky, herb-flecked squid to your favorite people, who couldn't be happier had you slaved at the stove all day long.

serves 4

Large pinch coarse kosher salt, plus more for the cooking water

1½ cups Israeli couscous

2½ tablespoons olive oil

1½ pounds squid, cut into ½-inch pieces and patted as dry as you can get it

3 tablespoons unsalted butter

2 tablespoons chopped fresh parsley

1 tablespoon chopped fresh basil

Large pinch (or two) crushed red pepper flakes

3 large garlic cloves, minced

Large pinch freshly ground black pepper

Freshly squeezed lemon juice, to taste

1. Bring a large pot of salted water to a boil. Add the couscous and cook until tender, 4 to 5 minutes. Drain well, toss with ½ tablespoon of the olive oil, and keep warm.

2. In a very large skillet over high heat, heat the remaining 2 tablespoons of oil until it begins to smoke. Carefully add the squid, butter, parsley, basil, red pepper flakes, and garlic (if your pan is small you may have to do this in two batches; you don't want it too full to toss). Cook, tossing frequently, until the squid is opaque and cooked through, 3 to 4 minutes. Season to taste with salt, black pepper, and lemon juice. Add the couscous to the pan and toss until incorporated.

Coconut fish stew with basil and lemongrass

My mother is the queen of doggie bags, so naturally, I've inherited some of the same urges. This is how I recently found myself staring into a partially consumed container of Thai takeout, wondering how I could metamorphose it into dinner.

Surprisingly, simmering that half quart of *tom yum*—the famous Thai hot-and-sour soup—with some plain white rice, leftover roast chicken, and a can of coconut milk made a sweet, sour, and very savory improvised stew. Of course the reason it was so easy was because the premade *tom yum* provided most of the complex flavor.

Wanting to re-create the dish, I turned to a simple *tom yum* recipe I found online. Unfortunately, it called for things far too exotic for my generally well-stocked greengrocer, including galangal and makrut lime. But with lemongrass in hand, I hoped substituting shallots, lime zest, and cilantro would create the aromatic Southeast Asian flavor I craved.

Once home, I made a quick broth, adding fish sauce for a salty depth and touches of brown sugar and rice vinegar. Then I threw in the fish, shrimp, and herbs, and let the flavors meld while the seafood cooked.

A few minutes later, my husband and I sat down to what turned out to be my favorite incarnation of my Thai-food experiments. Although it wasn't authentic, my latest stew was profoundly flavored, with pungent notes of herbs, lime, and saline fish sauce, softened by the creamy coconut milk, supple seafood, and rice. And I didn't even need leftovers as a head start.

serves 2

1 tablespoon vegetable oil

2 shallots, thinly sliced

1 small garlic clove, minced

2½ cups chicken broth

1 (13.5-ounce) can coconut milk

1 lemongrass stalk, finely chopped

1 jalapeño, seeded, if desired, thinly sliced

2 tablespoons rice vinegar

1 tablespoon Asian fish sauce, such as nam pla or nuoc mam

1 tablespoon light brown sugar

¾ teaspoon salt

Finely grated zest of 1 lime

¾ **pound seafood, such as snapper or other firm fish (cut into 1½-inch chunks), peeled shrimp, and/or scallops, or a combination**

2 tablespoons chopped fresh cilantro

2 tablespoons chopped fresh basil

Freshly squeezed lime juice, to taste

Cooked rice, for serving (optional)

(continued)

1. In a medium pot over medium heat, heat the oil. Add the shallots and garlic and cook, stirring, until the shallots are softened, 3 to 5 minutes. Stir in the broth, coconut milk, lemongrass, jalapeño, vinegar, fish sauce, brown sugar, salt, and lime zest. Simmer for 10 minutes.

2. Stir in the seafood and herbs. Cook for 2 to 3 minutes. Stir in the lime juice and serve with rice, if desired. (Without rice, it's more of a soup than a stew.)

Roasted blackfish with olives and sage

If you're not the type of cook who reels in her own catch, fish names make very little sense. And so it is with blackfish, a plump, pinkish-white fillet that I caught sight of at the fish stand at the farmers' market one day a few years back.

I'd never heard of blackfish, but I liked the look of the thick, pearly fillets, each large enough to feed two. A quick check on my Monterey Bay Aquarium Seafood Watch app confirmed they were sustainable, so I bought a large piece for dinner that night.

I cooked it simply, sautéing it in a little butter and lemon, and savored the fish's sweet ocean flavor, which was mild but very succulent. Since then, I've cooked blackfish every which way I can think of—seared, grilled, broiled, and roasted—and it is always good. As long as I don't overcook it, blackfish will adapt itself to my fishy whims.

And for a while, my whim was roasting. I love roasting fish because it's easy, only dirties one pan, and tends not to stink up the house as much as, say, stovetop grilling.

In this recipe, I top a couple of fillets with a little lemon, some earthy sage, and some sliced black olives (the only true black in the dish) that shrivel in the oven and give a perky, chewy, salty bite to the mellow, moon-white fish.

serves 4 to 6

3 tablespoons extra-virgin olive oil

2 (1-pound) skin-on blackfish fillets, patted dry

Kosher salt and freshly ground black pepper, to taste

Small bunch fresh sage

½ cup chopped pitted kalamata or other olives

Freshly squeezed juice of ½ lemon

Urfa or Aleppo pepper flakes (see Note, page 96), to taste

Best-quality extra-virgin olive oil, for drizzling (optional)

1. Preheat the oven to 425°F.

2. Drizzle 1 tablespoon of the olive oil over a rimmed baking sheet. Arrange the fish fillets, skin-side down, in the pan. Season the fish generously with salt and black pepper. Tear the sage leaves into small pieces and sprinkle them over the fish. Scatter the olives on top of and around the fish. Drizzle the fish with the remaining 2 tablespoons olive oil.

3. Transfer the pan to the oven and roast until the fish is just opaque, 8 to 10 minutes. Sprinkle the lemon juice over the fish and dust the fillets with Urfa or Aleppo pepper flakes. Finish with a light drizzle of best-quality olive oil, if desired.

Olive oil–poached halibut nuggets with garlic and mint

Eons ago, I went out with a man who lived near South Street Seaport. In the wee-hours, post-clubbing, we'd head to the Fulton Fish Market for late-night supper supplies.

Carl always used the same cooking technique no matter what fish we brought home: Melt several knobs of sweet butter in a cast-iron pan, then add the fish and cook it slowly until opaque but not brown at the edges. The trick was to keep the heat low enough that you don't fry the fish, but poach it gently in fat, keeping the flesh moist and velvety. Cutting the fish into cubes quickens the cooking time.

My love affair with Carl's fish recipe far outlasted that with the man, and I've adapted it widely over the years. I've swapped in olive oil, peanut oil, and even duck fat for the butter, and whole scallops and shrimp for the chunks of fish.

I especially like it with delicate whitefish that are prone to overcooking—halibut, for example, which requires focus to sear without drying it out. But slow poaching in lots of fat is forgiving. Even if it does go a minute longer than it should, it will stay supple.

For this recipe, I chose olive oil as the cooking medium because I had rosemary in the fridge and pairing the two is a classic. I also sprinkled some potent dried Turkish mint into the pan, along with garlic.

The halibut came out soft and juicy, infused with those heady flavors. A squeeze of lemon and some chopped fresh mint added brightness to this late-night-supper-turned-after-work meal, happily no clubbing required.

serves 2

1 pound halibut fillet, cut into 1¼-inch cubes

¼ teaspoon fine sea salt, plus more to taste

¼ teaspoon freshly ground black pepper, plus more to taste

¼ cup extra-virgin olive oil

1 small fresh rosemary sprig

½ teaspoon dried mint

2 garlic cloves, minced

Freshly squeezed lemon juice, to taste (optional)

Chopped fresh mint, for garnish

1. Season the halibut all over with a generous pinch each of salt and pepper.

(continued)

2. In a medium skillet (just large enough to hold the fish cubes in one layer but not much bigger) over low heat, heat the oil. Add the fish, rosemary sprig, and dried mint, and cook slowly until the fish begins to turn opaque, about 3 minutes. Stir in the garlic, salt, and pepper and cook until the garlic is fragrant and the fish is just cooked through, 3 minutes or so more (the heat should be low enough so as not to brown the garlic or fish, but high enough to gently cook everything; the cooking time will vary widely with your stove).

3. Taste and add more salt and pepper and a few drops of lemon juice, if desired. Stir in the fresh mint and serve, using a slotted spoon if you want to leave the poaching oil in the pan. But it's delicious over couscous or potatoes.

Steamed wild salmon with mustard greens, soy sauce, and ginger

Of all the fish I've come to love after a childhood of avoidance, cooked salmon was late to the table. Most of the cooked salmon I had been eating was overcooked and chalky. So for years I more or less restricted my salmon intake to smoked on bagels, cured as gravlax, or raw as sashimi or sushi.

But then one night I tasted a cooked salmon so moist and velvety, it flaked into large, soft chunks that melted like fish-flavored butter on the tongue, deep coral all the way through. It was from chef David Bouley, and his recipe said to wrap a heatproof plate of buttered salmon in plastic film, then let it cook in a 250°F oven (the plastic won't melt in such a low oven).

It became a regular part of my dinner-party rotation, the sauce changing to fit the seasons: sorrel in spring, rosemary and mushrooms in fall, and more.

But lately I've become far less enthused about wrapping my fish in potentially BPA-laden plastic. So instead, I decided to try steaming, since I'd had good success with a gently steamed flounder recipe once. Could the same technique work with salmon?

For once I followed my own recipe, sautéing the mustard greens with the garlic and ginger, and adding soy sauce and sesame oil for a nutty, salty tang. Then, instead of flounder, I plopped salmon on top and covered the skillet to trap the steam. A few minutes later, I had soft, sweet, just-cooked fish on top of pungent greens: cooked salmon that even I can love.

serves 2

1 tablespoon vegetable or peanut oil

1 teaspoon toasted (Asian) sesame oil, plus more for drizzling

3 garlic cloves, minced

1 (1-inch-thick) slice fresh ginger, peeled and minced

1 very large or 2 small bunches mustard greens, stems removed and leaves torn into pieces

1 tablespoon soy sauce (if using tamari or double soy sauce, use a little less), plus more for drizzling

2 (6- to 8-ounce) wild salmon fillets

Kosher salt and freshly ground black pepper, to taste

1. In a very large skillet over medium-high heat, heat the oils. Add the garlic and ginger and sauté until fragrant and translucent, about 2 minutes. Add the mustard greens, soy sauce, and 3 tablespoons water and sauté until the greens start to wilt, 2 minutes more.

2. Spread the greens out in the bottom of the pan. Season the salmon with salt and pepper and place it on top of the greens. Cover the pan, reduce the heat to medium, and let the fish steam until just cooked through, about 6 minutes. If the pan dries out before the fish is cooked through, add a little more water, a teaspoon at a time.

3. Uncover the pan and transfer the fish to serving plates. If the greens seem wet, increase the heat to high to cook off any excess moisture. Serve the greens on top of the fish, drizzled with a little more sesame oil and soy sauce, if desired.

Thai-style ground turkey with chiles and basil

I have a hard time categorizing this savory, zesty, garlicky dish. It's a bit like a sloppy joe without the tomatoes or bread, or maybe vaguely like an aromatic, beanless, thinner-sauced turkey chili. It's as quick to make as a stir-fry and employs the same technique, but I don't usually associate stir-fries with nubby ground meat. Call it what you will, it's one of my favorite easy dinners to throw together when I'm in the mood for a punchy, Thai-inflected meal but want something more wholesome and homemade than takeout.

And it really is easy, which is what you want when August's heat has rendered you unable to do much other than sit languorously in front of the computer. The hardest thing about this dish is assembling the ingredients—not that they are difficult to find, it's just that there are a lot of them. But once you've got everything lined up on the counter, your dinner will come together in minutes, without having the stove on very long when the last thing you want is to heat up the kitchen even more than Mother Nature (or is it the god of climate change?) has seen fit to do for you.

Of course, even if you made this in the winter, its flavors would be utterly mouth-watering. It's a craveable mix of fragrant lime, funky fish sauce, and plenty of ginger and garlic that livens up the blank canvas that is ground turkey in an entirely new way.

serves 4

1 tablespoon soy sauce

About 1 tablespoon Asian fish sauce, such as nam pla or nuoc mam, or to taste

¼ teaspoon finely grated lime zest

1 teaspoon freshly squeezed lime juice

½ teaspoon sugar

1 tablespoon peanut oil

1 tablespoon finely chopped peeled fresh ginger

3 garlic cloves, finely chopped

1 jalapeño, seeded and finely chopped

1 fat scallion, white and light green parts finely chopped, greens sliced and reserved for garnish

1 pound ground turkey

½ cup chopped fresh Thai or regular basil

Coconut Rice (page 144—omit the peas) or cooked regular rice, for serving

Lime wedges, for serving

1. In a small bowl, whisk together the soy sauce, fish sauce, lime zest, lime juice, and sugar. (If you think your fish sauce is very salty, start with 2 teaspoons; you can add more at the end if the dish needs it.)

2. In a large skillet over medium-high heat, heat the oil. Add the ginger, garlic, jalapeño, and chopped scallion white and light green parts. Cook, stirring, until slightly softened, about a minute. Stir in the turkey. Cook the meat, breaking it up with a fork, until it is no longer pink, 5 to 7 minutes.

3. Stir in the soy sauce mixture and cook for a minute or so, until the flavors come together. Remove from the heat and stir in the basil. Scatter with the sliced scallion greens. Serve, over warm coconut or regular rice, with lime wedges on the side.

Spicy three-meat chili

Daniel's favorite dish is chili. Whenever I ask him what he wants for dinner, chili is nearly always the answer, no matter the season. I make it in the winter, when it's frigid and foul. I make it in the spring, when it's rainy and raw. I even make it in the summer on the hottest, steamiest days. But autumn seems to me to be the ideal chili-cooking time of year, when the weather is cold enough to warrant long, savory simmering, and you still might be able to snag the last of the bell peppers or jalapeños at the farmers' market.

Daniel is a chili enthusiast of the most democratic ilk. As long as it's stewy, spicy, and filled with lots of little tasty tidbits to munch, he will finish the bowl and lick the spoon.

I'm a lot pickier, avoiding situations where I am forced, out of politeness, to consume vegetarian chili, tofu chili, or chili made from anything with wings.

This chili satisfies us both. The trio of meats gives it a complex, interesting flavor— sweet from the veal, brawny from the pork, and robust from the beef—and we both like the combination of fresh chiles and dried chili powder, and all the vegetables and beans for textural amusement.

Unfortunately, Dahlia, as of now, doesn't like chili at all. We assume one day that will change, and, until then, she'll have plenty of opportunities to try the dish again and again, year in and year out.

serves 8

1 tablespoon extra-virgin olive oil

1 pound ground beef or bison

2½ teaspoons kosher salt, plus more to taste

1½ teaspoons freshly ground black pepper, plus more to taste

1 pound ground pork

1 pound ground veal

1½ tablespoons tomato paste

1 medium green bell pepper, diced

1 medium red bell pepper, diced

1 medium onion, finely chopped

2 garlic cloves, finely chopped

1 to 2 jalapeños, to taste, seeded and finely chopped

3 tablespoons chili powder, plus more to taste

1 (28-ounce) can crushed tomatoes

1 (28-ounce) can whole peeled tomatoes, broken up with a fork

3 cups cooked kidney beans, or 2 (15-ounce) cans, drained and rinsed

Chopped fresh cilantro, for serving

Lime wedges, for serving

1. In a large pot over medium-high heat, heat the oil. Add the beef and cook, breaking it up with a fork, until well browned, 5 to 7 minutes. Season the meat with ½ teaspoon each of the salt and black pepper. Remove the beef with a slotted spoon and transfer the meat to a paper towel–lined platter. Repeat the cooking process twice more with the pork and veal. Season each with ½ teaspoon of the salt and pepper.

2. Add the tomato paste to the pot. Cook, stirring, until the paste is golden brown, 1 to 2 minutes. Stir in the bell peppers, onion, garlic, and jalapeño. Cook until the vegetables are softened, 7 to 10 minutes. Stir in the chili powder and a pinch of salt; cook for 1 minute. Add the tomatoes, beans, 2 cups water, and the remaining 1 teaspoon salt. Return the meat to the pot. Reduce the heat to medium and simmer for 30 minutes.

3. Ladle the chili into bowls. Sprinkle with cilantro and serve with lime wedges.

Stir-fried chicken with leeks, oyster mushrooms, and peanuts

As much as I've loved Chinese takeout food—the cheap, filling, completely inauthentic stuff I used to have delivered from my neighborhood joint on a regular basis—I recently gave it up. I've become horrified by what I assume is a meal composed of factory-farm chicken and CAFO beef. Not to say I'm a total purist when it comes to meats, but giving up meaty stir-fries in takeout Chinese? That I can do.

So these days, when I get a hankering for inauthentic Chinese food, I scratch the itch by making it myself.

And here's what I've learned, something I've long known in theory but never really lived: Stir-fries are easy. They are quick. The hardest part is cutting up the ingredients, but once that is done, dinner practically is, too.

In this recipe, I use humanely raised boneless chicken thighs (breasts also work if you like white meat), marinated in soy sauce, rice vinegar, and sesame oil to give them a deep, nutty flavor. Then I add mushrooms and leeks to the pan as the vegetable factor. (Stir-fries always need a vegetable factor.) Mushrooms work especially well because they add a meaty character that deepens the flavor of the chicken. Then I garnish everything with loads of chopped peanuts for crunch and a shower of cilantro for a fresh, herby flavor. Together they help make a dish that's a cut above the usual takeout, in so many ways.

serves 2 or 3

2 tablespoons soy sauce (less if you are using dark soy or tamari, which are stronger)

2 tablespoons rice vinegar, plus more for serving

1½ tablespoons toasted (Asian) sesame oil

2 teaspoons light brown sugar or granulated sugar

¾ pound boneless, skinless chicken breasts or thighs, cut crosswise into ½-inch strips

2 tablespoons finely chopped peeled fresh ginger

2 garlic cloves, finely chopped

3 tablespoons peanut oil

½ pound oyster mushrooms, sliced ½ inch thick

2 to 3 leeks, white and light green parts only, cleaned and thinly sliced (see Note, page 50)

Pinch kosher salt (optional)

3 tablespoons finely chopped peanuts

2 tablespoons chopped fresh cilantro

Steamed rice, for serving

1. In a small bowl, whisk together the soy sauce, vinegar, sesame oil, and brown sugar. In a large bowl, combine the chicken with half the marinade (reserve the other half for stir-frying) and half the chopped ginger and garlic. Cover the chicken with plastic wrap and refrigerate for at least 30 minutes and up to 2 hours (longer than that and the chicken will get mushy).

2. Heat a large 12-inch or so skillet over the highest heat until the pan is screaming hot, about 5 minutes. Add 1 tablespoon of the peanut oil and tilt the skillet so that the bottom is evenly coated with the oil. Lift the chicken from the marinade (shake off any excess liquid) and add it to the hot skillet. Cook, stirring constantly and quickly, until the chicken is just cooked through, about 2 minutes for breasts and 3 to 4 minutes for thigh meat. Transfer the chicken to a plate.

3. Add the remaining 2 tablespoons of peanut oil to the skillet. Add the mushrooms and cook, stirring constantly, until the mushrooms are browned and soft, 2 to 3 minutes. Add the leeks and cook until wilted, about 1 minute. Stir in the reserved marinade. Push the vegetables to the border of the pan, leaving an open space in the middle. Add the remaining chopped ginger and garlic to the open space. Mash it around with your spoon until it is tender and fragrant, about 30 seconds. Return the chicken to the pan and quickly toss it with the ginger, garlic, and vegetables. Taste and add a pinch of salt if it needs it.

4. Remove the pan from the heat and toss in the peanuts and cilantro. Mound the stir-fry over steamed rice, and sprinkle judiciously with rice vinegar before serving.

Roasted chicken thighs with apples, gin, and coriander seeds

The beauty of this recipe is not just the gorgeous melding of flavors, but how quickly and easily I can throw it together all year round. Cut into finger-size strips, the chicken and very thinly sliced apples cook in only twenty minutes, during which time they miraculously produce a pan sauce that is fragrant and heady.

Even better, that sauce results from just a few kitchen staples. Along with the requisite garlic, olive oil, salt, and pepper, I added cilantro, an herb I adore year in and out. Then from the spice cabinet, I pulled out the coriander seeds, which I had no doubt would go perfectly well with the cilantro.

I tipped in some vermouth from the too-tall bottle in the fridge, and was about to stick everything in the oven when I started to worry that the subtle flavor of vermouth wouldn't be lively enough to lift the dish. Then I remembered the words of my father when he counseled me on zipping up a scallop pan roast.

"Gin," he said, "makes everything taste better."

And it is certainly on friendly terms with vermouth. So I added a few drops.

Soon the kitchen was enveloped in an apple-and-curry-spice perfume. The dish was exotic and fragrant, with the coriander seeds adding a pleasing crunch against the tender apples. Twenty minutes in the oven created a martini-like alchemy, just right for dinner.

serves 2 or 3

1 large or 2 small apples

1 pound boneless, skinless chicken thighs, cut into 1-inch strips

2 tablespoons extra-virgin olive oil

1 tablespoon white vermouth

1½ teaspoons gin

2 tablespoons chopped fresh cilantro, dill, or parsley

2 garlic cloves, minced

1 teaspoon coriander seeds

½ teaspoon kosher salt

½ teaspoon freshly ground black pepper

Crusty bread or cooked rice, for serving

1. Preheat the oven to 400°F.

2. Core the apples and slice them as thinly as you can without getting out (or buying!) a mandoline (between ⅛ and ¼ inch is fine).

3. In a 9 × 13-inch pan, toss all the ingredients except 1 tablespoon of the cilantro (or dill or parsley). Spread the ingredients into one layer in the pan. Roast until the chicken is cooked through and the apples are softened, about 20 minutes. Garnish with the reserved cilantro (or dill or parsley). The sauce will be thin, so serve with crusty bread or over rice to sop up the sauce.

Crisp roasted chicken with chickpeas, lemons, and carrots with parsley gremolata

When I flip through food magazines, I rarely read the recipes. I look at the photos and imagine what I think the recipe should be. Most of the time I get it pretty close, but sometimes I'm way off base. This recipe is an example of that.

The photo was of a roasted chicken on a bed of crunchy, salty chickpeas and what I thought were tiny cubes of melting carrot. But, in fact, the carrots turned out to be bits of orange bell pepper and the chickpeas were added to the pan last minute so they would stay moist and soft. I'm sure it was a perfectly good dish, but I liked my own idea better.

So the next time I roasted a chicken, I placed it on a rack over chickpeas and carrot slices so all the good juices would drip down onto them. I added slivered lemon because it caramelizes when roasted and would perk up the garam masala, a spicy, earthy Indian spice blend I rubbed on the bird.

While it roasted, I chopped together a mix of parsley, lemon zest, and garlic (known as gremolata) to sprinkle on top for a little kick, which would be welcome with all the hearty flavors.

The finished chicken was burnished, the chickpeas, lemon bits, and carrots caramelized and tender—overall, intensely lemony and very succulent. Maybe one day I'll dig up that other recipe to give it a whirl . . . though given how delightful this dish is, maybe not.

serves 4

FOR THE CHICKEN

2 lemons

2 (15-ounce) cans chickpeas, drained, or 3½ cups cooked chickpeas

2 tablespoons extra-virgin olive oil

1½ tablespoons garam masala

3 teaspoons kosher salt

1½ teaspoons freshly ground black pepper

1 (3½-pound) whole chicken, patted dry

4 fresh thyme sprigs

3 tablespoons unsalted butter, at room temperature

1 pound carrots, cut into 1-inch rounds

FOR THE GREMOLATA

3 tablespoons chopped fresh parsley

½ teaspoon finely grated lemon zest

1 small garlic clove, finely chopped

(continued)

1. MAKE THE CHICKEN: Preheat the oven to 400°F.

2. Quarter the lemons lengthwise and remove and discard any seeds. Thinly slice 6 of the lemon quarters crosswise (you will get little triangles) and in a bowl, toss them with the chickpeas, oil, ½ tablespoon (which equals 1½ teaspoons if you don't have a ½-tablespoon measure) of the garam masala, 1 teaspoon of the salt, and ½ teaspoon of the pepper.

3. Season the inside of the chicken cavity with 1 teaspoon of the salt and ½ teaspoon of the pepper. Fill the cavity with the remaining lemon wedges and the thyme sprigs. Rub the outside of the chicken all over with the remaining 1 tablespoon garam masala, 1 teaspoon salt, and ½ teaspoon pepper. Rub the butter all over the skin.

4. Scatter the carrots in the bottom of the largest roasting pan you have (the one you use for your Thanksgiving turkey). Place a wire roasting rack over the carrots; arrange the chicken, breast-side up, on the rack. Transfer the pan to the oven and roast, stirring the carrots occasionally, for 30 minutes. Scatter the chickpea mixture into the bottom of the roasting pan. Continue to roast until the chicken's thigh juices run clear when pierced with a knife, 45 to 60 minutes more. Let the chicken rest for 5 minutes before carving.

5. MEANWHILE, MAKE THE GREMOLATA: Combine the parsley, lemon zest, and garlic in a bowl.

6. Spoon the carrot-chickpea mixture onto a platter; arrange the chicken on top. Sprinkle the gremolata over the dish and serve.

Seared pork chops with kimchi

Some people collect stamps, others vintage bartender guides or mounted rare butterflies. Me, I'm cultivating a prodigious collection of condiments that's slowly taking over the entirety of the fridge, much to my husband's dismay. Every few years, I'm forced to downsize, clearing the way to let in the new. And in an effort to use up some things, I rediscovered kimchi, a potent, mouth-searing Korean condiment made from fermented cabbage, garlic, and chiles.

At Korean restaurants, it's often an accompaniment, but I wanted its peppery pungency to be more integrated into a main dish.

So I decided to try rubbing chopped-up kimchi all over some pork chops, then pan-frying them.

I thought this would be a fine idea. But once I took my golden brown chops out of the skillet, most of the kimchi—along with its vibrant flavor—remained behind. The easiest solution was to make a little kimchi pan sauce.

To deglaze the pan, I added a splash of dry vermouth and simmered it down, but somehow the alcohol intensified the kimchi, making it even more assertive and biting than before—maybe a little *too* biting, I thought, as I squinted through the sourness.

So I tossed in a big lump of butter and a squirt of honey to tame the aggressive flavors, mellowing the harshness while allowing the racy garlic and chile notes to enliven the meaty pork. The dish was so good that my husband, noticing the empty kimchi container, told me later that he even contemplated suggesting we stock up. But then, unable to fit the leftovers into the fridge, he didn't.

serves 2

4 (1-inch-thick) bone-in pork chops	½ cup white wine or vermouth
6 tablespoons chopped kimchi (sold in Asian markets)	1 to 2 teaspoons honey, or to taste
1 tablespoon olive oil	1 tablespoon unsalted butter
	Chopped scallions, for garnish

1. Smear the pork chops with 2 tablespoons of the kimchi, cover, and refrigerate for at least 30 minutes and up to 24 hours (the longer, the better).

2. Wipe off the pork to remove the pieces of clinging kimchi, and add those pieces to the remaining 4 tablespoons kimchi. In a large skillet over high heat, heat the oil. Sear the pork until golden brown on both sides, about 3 minutes a side. Reduce the

(continued)

heat to low and cook the pork until done to taste, about 7 minutes more, turning once. Transfer the pork to a plate and cover with foil to keep warm.

3. Add the wine or vermouth, 1 teaspoon of the honey, and the kimchi to the skillet. Raise the heat to high and simmer, scraping up the browned bits from the bottom of the pan, until almost all the liquid has evaporated, about 3 minutes. Whisk in the butter. Taste and add more honey, if needed; the sauce should be tart but not puckery.

4. Serve the pork chops coated with the sauce and garnished with scallions.

Braised pork shoulder with tomatoes, cinnamon, and olives over polenta

This is exactly the right kind of savory, warming dish to bring to a friend who is feeling unwell. In my case, it was for Josh, who was just back home from the hospital after being hit by a car while riding his bike. His wrist was smashed to bits and his spirit was shaken.

I had volunteered to bring him dinner. So I wandered the farmers' market stalls that morning, looking for inspiration, which unveiled itself to me in the form of a small chunk of pork shoulder. Offering various shoulders—to cry on, to eat—to Josh and family seemed apropos for this particular situation, so I snapped it right up.

With a pork shoulder in the bag, a cook has options. I could have roasted it, but a braise is easier to transport and reheat.

For the seasonings, I wanted to simmer up something comforting but different, something vaguely exotic that would taste of sunny, faraway places where no one ever drove SUVs at top speed down residential streets.

I doubt this place exists, but if it does, I'm sure they use plenty of dry red wine and sweet spices in their braises, along with anchovies for complexity, and tart olives and those canned plum tomatoes I had in the cupboard as a bright contrast.

I cooked it carefully and brought it over to Josh's house with some freshly made polenta and a chilled bottle of Champagne. Because this dinner was a celebration—of luck, pork, dedicated bike lanes, and, most important, eating good food with dear friends.

serves 4 to 6

2 pounds boneless pork shoulder (also called pork butt), cut into 2-inch chunks

Kosher salt and freshly ground black pepper, to taste

2 tablespoons olive oil

2 large leeks, white and light green parts only, cleaned and sliced (see Note, page 50)

5 garlic cloves, smashed and peeled

1 (28-ounce) can plum tomatoes

1 cup dry red wine

5 anchovies

1 (2-inch) piece cinnamon stick

2 bay leaves

2 fresh rosemary sprigs

⅔ cup coarsely chopped pitted green olives

Cooked polenta (see page 84), for serving

1. Preheat the oven to 300°F.

2. Season the pork shoulder generously with salt and pepper. In a Dutch oven over medium-high heat, warm the olive oil and sear the pork, turning, until it is well browned all over, about 10 minutes. Transfer the pork to a plate.

3. Add the leeks and garlic to the Dutch oven and cook, stirring, for 3 to 5 minutes.

4. Return the pork to the Dutch oven and add the tomatoes with their liquid, wine, anchovies, cinnamon stick, bay leaves, and rosemary. Cover the Dutch oven and place it in the oven. Cook for 1½ to 2 hours, turning the pork twice during cooking (once after 45 minutes and again after 1½ hours).

5. Increase the oven temperature to 425°F. Uncover the Dutch oven and add the olives. Continue cooking, uncovered, until the liquid has reduced and the meat is very tender, about 20 minutes more. If you have made this ahead of time, let it cool so the fat has a chance to rise to the surface, then spoon it off if you like (I usually don't bother). If you've made it the day before, chilling hardens the fat and makes it really easy to spoon off. Reheat if necessary and serve over polenta.

Lamb merguez burgers with harissa mayonnaise

There is a minimalist elegance to a good hamburger. Simply seasoned with salt and pepper and grilled to medium-rare perfection, it needs nothing more than a soft white bun, though an assortment of tasty accoutrements can only make things better—if you're the burger-topping type.

At the other end of the spectrum is my spicy lamb burger. Imbued with coriander, fennel, cayenne, and plenty of onion and garlic, it's got the same flavor profile as a merguez sausage in a burger-patty package. When served charred on the outside and juicy within, it is bold, intense, deeply savory, and as far from minimalist as you can get, in the best possible way.

I like to serve it in a whole wheat pita pocket swathed in harissa mayonnaise and piled high with crunchy vegetables. But the fiery, gamy flavors of chile and lamb can easily stand alone on the plate—before you come along to gobble it up.

serves 4

½ teaspoon coriander seeds

½ teaspoon fennel seeds

1 pound ground lamb

¼ cup finely chopped onion

2 tablespoons cold unsalted butter, cut into small pieces

2 garlic cloves, finely chopped

1½ teaspoons kosher salt

1 teaspoon paprika

Pinch cayenne

Olive oil, for brushing

⅓ cup mayonnaise

1½ teaspoons harissa, or to taste

4 whole wheat or regular pita breads

Sliced cucumber, for serving

Sliced tomatoes, for serving

Salad greens, for serving

1. In a dry skillet over medium heat, toast the coriander and fennel until fragrant. Transfer the spices to a spice grinder and finely grind (alternatively, you can use a mortar and pestle).

2. In a large bowl, mix together the ground spices, lamb, onion, butter, garlic, salt, paprika, and cayenne until just combined. Form into 4 equal-size patties, about ¾ inch thick.

3. Preheat a grill to medium-high. Brush the grate lightly with oil. Place the burgers on the grill. Close the cover and cook to the desired doneness, about 3 minutes per side for medium-rare. Let the burgers rest for 5 minutes before serving.

4. In a small bowl, whisk together the mayonnaise and harissa; taste and add more harissa if desired. Spoon the harissa mayo into the pitas. Fill the pitas with the burgers, cucumber, tomatoes, and greens and serve immediately.

Braised leg of lamb with garlicky root vegetable puree

Because I grew up spending Christmas Eve in Chinatown with my clan of New York City Jews, I wasn't wedded to any one particular tradition when celebrating the holiday. But when Daniel moved in, we wanted to create new holiday traditions together.

One of them has become braising a large hunk of meat. For our family, it's the ideal holiday dish. We can braise it in advance, serve it to friends on Christmas Eve, then reheat the leftovers for Christmas dinner, when we are too tired from opening presents and our annual Christmas walk around the park (one of my new favorite traditions) to want to cook anything new.

We've varied the contents of the braising pot over the years, but keep coming back to leg of lamb because we both love it, and since we don't eat it very often, it seems like a special meal. Plus, braising a bone-in leg of lamb is an excellent way to cook it. The marrow flows into the sauce, thickening and seasoning it, while the meat collapses and becomes spoonably soft.

In this recipe, I've added anchovy and olives to the pot to give the sauce a tangy depth that works well with all the rich meat. It's especially nice served over a smooth, sweet root vegetable puree spiked with garlic that acts like a velvety sauce. On Christmas Day, we toss the leftovers with pasta. It's a wonderful new two-day tradition, boiled down into one pot.

serves 6

FOR THE LAMB

1 (4½-pound) bone-in shank end leg of lamb, rinsed and patted dry

3 tablespoons olive oil

1 tablespoon plus ¼ teaspoon kosher salt

1¾ teaspoons freshly ground black pepper

2 cups chicken broth

1 (750-ml) bottle fruity white wine

3 small onions (¾ pound), halved and thinly sliced

3 large carrots (¾ pound), sliced into ½-inch rounds

1 large parsnip (¼ pound), sliced into ½-inch rounds

4 anchovy fillets

2 fresh rosemary sprigs

2 fresh sage or thyme sprigs

1 bay leaf

½ cup coarsely chopped pitted green olives

FOR THE GARLICKY ROOT VEGETABLE PUREE

1 large celeriac bulb, peeled and diced

2 medium Yukon Gold potatoes, diced

2 large parsnips, diced

4 garlic cloves

2 bay leaves

2 tablespoons plus 1 teaspoon kosher salt, plus more to taste

½ cup (1 stick) unsalted butter

Freshly grated nutmeg, to taste

2 garlic cloves, finely chopped

¼ teaspoon kosher salt

1. MAKE THE LAMB: Preheat the oven to 450°F.

2. Rub the lamb with 1 tablespoon of the oil and season it with 1 tablespoon of the salt and 1½ teaspoons of the pepper.

3. In a medium saucepan over medium-high heat, bring the broth and wine to a boil; allow it to bubble gently and reduce while you sauté the vegetables, about 10 minutes or so.

4. In a large Dutch oven over medium-high heat, warm the remaining 2 tablespoons of oil. Add the onions and cook, stirring occasionally, until soft, 7 to 10 minutes. Stir in the carrots, parsnip, anchovies, remaining ¼ teaspoon salt, remaining ¼ teaspoon pepper, the rosemary, sage, and bay leaf. Turn off the heat and pour in just enough of the broth-wine mixture to cover the vegetables. Place the lamb, fatty-side up, on top of the vegetables.

5. Transfer the pot to the oven and cook, uncovered, for 25 minutes. Then add the remaining broth, cover the pot, and reduce the oven temperature to 325°F. Cook for 1½ hours at a bare simmer, reducing the oven temperature if necessary, then turn the lamb over. Cook for 1½ hours more and turn the lamb over again. Uncover the pot and stir in the olives. Cook for another hour, turning the lamb after 30 minutes. At this point the lamb should be soft enough to cut with a serving spoon. If not, cover the pot and continue to cook until it is.

6. MAKE THE ROOT VEGETABLE PUREE: In a large saucepan, combine the celery root, potatoes, parsnips, garlic cloves, and bay leaves. Pour in 12 cups water and 2 tablespoons of the salt. Bring to a boil over medium-high heat; reduce the heat, and simmer until tender, 20 to 25 minutes. Drain, discard the bay leaves, and transfer the root vegetables and garlic to a food processor. Add the butter, remaining teaspoon salt, and the nutmeg; process until very smooth. Taste and add more salt if necessary. Keep warm or reheat before serving.

7. Just before serving, mash the finely chopped garlic and the salt to form a paste. Stir it into the lamb's pan juices.

8. To serve, make a bed of the root vegetable puree on each plate. Cut the lamb with a serving spoon and lay some of it over the puree, along with some vegetables and garlicky pan juices.

Vietnamese grilled steak and cabbage salad with peanuts, mint, and chiles

By the time April rolls around, I'm ready to be done with cabbage. That's when I know it's time for a new recipe, something slightly out of my Eastern European comfort zone, to whet my appetite and get me back into a cabbage groove.

Whenever I start to get that winter palate fatigue, my best cure is usually a dish inspired by more temperate climes, places rich with spunky spice and heat and plenty of lively citrus.

One thought was to take a mental trip to a place I've been to in restaurants only: Vietnam. I remembered a cabbage salad spiked with chile, garlic, fish sauce, limes, and herbs that I often order.

There were hundreds of renditions on the Internet, some with meat, some without. Since I was looking for dinner, I cherry-picked from the selections, adding and subtracting ingredients to match what I had in the fridge and freezer (namely, a flank steak), and what I could easily pick up at the store around the corner (ginger, lime, cilantro, but not lemongrass).

I made a pungent marinade for the steak, and while it marinated I whisked together a vibrant soy sauce–based vinaigrette and tossed it with the shredded cabbage. The dressing was so bright and flavorful it immediately made me overcome any cabbage inhibitions, and I inhaled half the bowl before I remembered that there were also some nice slices of bloody steak on my plate, too. It was a perfect winter-doldrums meal that made spring seem not so very far away after all.

serves 4

¼ cup soy sauce

Finely grated zest and freshly squeezed juice of 1 lime

2 tablespoons grated fresh peeled ginger

2 teaspoons toasted (Asian) sesame oil

2 garlic cloves, finely chopped

1 (¼-pound) flank steak, rinsed and patted dry

2 carrots

10 cups shredded napa or regular cabbage (about ½ head)

¼ cup chopped fresh cilantro (or mint or basil)

Kosher salt and freshly ground black pepper, to taste

2 tablespoons chopped unsalted peanuts (optional)

(continued)

2 tablespoons soy sauce

1 tablespoon rice vinegar

2 tablespoons extra-virgin olive or peanut oil

1 teaspoon Asian fish sauce, such as nam pla or nuoc mam

Freshly squeezed juice of 1 lime, plus more as needed

Pinch cayenne

1 garlic clove, finely chopped

1. In a medium bowl, whisk together the soy sauce, lime zest and juice, ginger, and sesame oil. On a cutting board, use the flat side of a knife to mash the garlic into a paste (or use a mortar and pestle). Whisk the garlic paste into the marinade. Place the steak in a shallow dish and cover with the marinade, turning completely to coat. Cover the dish with plastic wrap and refrigerate for at least 1 hour and up to 12 hours. Remove the steak from the refrigerator 30 minutes prior to cooking.

2. In a food processor fitted with the large grating attachment, shred the carrots. Turn them out into a large bowl. Add the cabbage and cilantro. Toss well. Cover tightly with plastic wrap and refrigerate for up to 3 hours.

3. MAKE THE VINAIGRETTE: In a small bowl, whisk together the soy sauce, vinegar, olive or peanut oil, fish sauce, lime juice, and cayenne. On a cutting board, use the flat side of a knife to mash the garlic into a paste (or use a mortar and pestle). Whisk the garlic paste into the vinaigrette.

4. Preheat the broiler and position a rack in the top third of the oven.

5. Remove the steak from the marinade, scraping off any excess, and season with salt and pepper. Transfer the steak to a baking sheet. Broil, turning once halfway through, until browned, about 3 minutes per side for medium-rare. Transfer the steak to a cutting board and let rest for 5 minutes. Thinly slice the steak against the grain.

6. To assemble, add just enough of the vinaigrette to the salad to coat it and toss well. Taste and add more dressing or salt or lime juice if desired. Place the salad onto the center of a platter and top with the steak. Sprinkle with the chopped peanuts, if desired, drizzle with more vinaigrette, and serve.

Chile-coconut braised beef short ribs

When Dahlia turned one, Daniel and I decided we wanted to have professional pictures taken of our little family. So I asked our friend and neighbor Lucy Schaeffer, one of the most talented food photographers out there, if she'd be interested in trading a family photo session for a catered dinner made by me.

This chile-flecked, creamy, slow-cooked beef dish is what she chose out of a long list of entrée possibilities.

Now, here is a confession. When I sent her the entrée ideas, I'd never made any of them before. I chose braised meats as a focus, since they are easy to make in advance and deliver to your neighbor's door without losing anything in the journey.

I knew I wanted the beef to be very succulent, so I bought boneless short ribs and cut them into large cubes. As they cooked in a mixture of coconut milk, chiles, and spices, the whole house filled with rich and meaty aromas and Daniel started asking me when dinner would be ready. Sadly, I had to tell him that we were eating pasta. The beef was for Lucy's family.

When it was ready, Daniel and I stole a few pieces of meat before forcing ourselves to pack up the rest of it. Then I made the dish all over again the very next day. The second batch tasted even better to us, though anticipation might have had something to do with that.

serves 6

2 pounds boneless beef short ribs, cut into 2-inch chunks

1½ teaspoons kosher salt, plus more to taste

1 teaspoon chili powder (hot or mild)

½ teaspoon freshly ground black pepper, plus more to taste

1 tablespoon coconut oil or olive oil

4 garlic cloves, minced

2 jalapeños, seeded, if desired, and minced

1 (2-inch) piece fresh ginger, peeled and grated

1 small shallot, minced

½ teaspoon cumin seeds

1 (13.5-ounce) can coconut milk

Finely grated zest and freshly squeezed juice of 2 limes

Chopped fresh cilantro, for serving

Chopped scallions, for serving

Lime wedges, for serving (optional)

Coconut Rice with Optional Peas (page 144), if desired

(continued)

1. Preheat the oven to 325°F.

2. Season the beef all over with 1 teaspoon of the salt, the chili powder, and the pepper. In a 5-quart Dutch oven over medium-high heat, heat the oil. Add the beef and cook until browned all over, about 8 minutes. Add the garlic, jalapeños, ginger, shallot, and cumin seeds and cook, stirring, until everything is fragrant and golden, about 2 minutes more.

3. Stir in the coconut milk, lime zest and juice, remaining ½ teaspoon salt, pepper to taste, and ½ cup water. Bring the liquid to a simmer, then cover and transfer the pot to the oven. Cook until the beef is very tender, 2 to 2½ hours, turning the meat after an hour.

4. Serve with coconut rice, if you like, garnished with cilantro and scallions, and have lime wedges on the side for squeezing, if desired.

dinner
sides

Homemade spaetzle with browned onions, Swiss chard, and Emmentaler

When my ex-husband and I broke up, our annual beer-and-mulled-wine-fueled Oktoberfest parties ceased, and so I stopped making spaetzle, tiny egg-rich dumplings topped with browned onions and cheese. It was too much work anyway, I thought, requiring too many hands—one pair to hold the colander over the boiling water, one pair to pour the batter into the colander, and one pair to constantly stir the water receiving the spaetzle drips.

But then one day my cousins sent me a gift from their travels in Germany: a shiny stainless steel spaetzle maker, the kind that sits on top of the pot of boiling water. Now I could make the spaetzle all by myself, so I did.

While I caramelized the onions, I rifled through the fridge, looking for something to make into a salad. A dish this rich needs something green to eat alongside. There were no salad greens or cucumbers, but there was a bushy bunch of dark green Swiss chard. I could throw that into the pan with the onions and get my green and my gooey cheese in the same bite. And Swiss chard would surely go well with the Swiss Emmentaler cheese I was using.

I tried it, adding the chard to the pan to wilt with the onions, then stirring the mixture into the homemade spaetzle. Then I baked everything until the cheese was bubbling and browned on top.

Two friends and I devoured the spaetzle hot from the oven. And this time, instead of beer, we washed it down with crisp white wine.

serves 6 to 8 as a side dish, 4 as an main course

1½ tablespoons unsalted butter

1 large Spanish onion, halved and thinly sliced

1 large fresh thyme sprig

1 teaspoon plus 1 pinch kosher salt, plus more as needed

1 small bunch Swiss chard or beet greens, stems removed and leaves cut into pieces

2¼ cups all-purpose flour

¼ teaspoon freshly grated nutmeg

2 large eggs, lightly beaten

¾ cup milk

2 cups grated Emmentaler or Gruyère cheese (about 8 ounces)

1. In a large skillet over medium-high heat, melt the butter and add the onion and thyme, stirring briefly to coat with the butter. Cook the onion, without stirring, until it starts to get dark brown, then add a pinch of salt and stir occasionally until the onion is tender and caramelized, about 30 minutes total.

2. Stir in the Swiss chard or beet greens and cook until tender, 3 to 5 minutes, then transfer the mixture to a large bowl.

3. Preheat the oven to 375°F. Bring a large pot of salted water to a boil.

4. To make the spaetzle, combine the flour, nutmeg, and remaining 1 teaspoon salt in a large bowl. In a separate bowl, whisk together the eggs and milk. Make a well in the dry ingredients and pour in the egg mixture. Mix well with a wooden spoon.

5. Fill a large bowl with ice water and keep it nearby. Place the dough in a spaetzle maker over the pot of boiling water. Shave the dough into the water (alternatively, push the dough through a colander into the water). When the dumplings rise to the surface, use a slotted spoon to transfer them to the bowl of ice water.

6. Drain the spaetzle well and transfer to the bowl with the onions and greens. Sprinkle in three-quarters of the cheese and mix to combine.

7. Scrape the spaetzle mixture into a 2-quart gratin dish, sprinkle on the remaining cheese, and bake for 25 to 30 minutes, until the top is golden brown and bubbling. Serve immediately.

Coconut rice with optional peas

In our house, coconut rice is like magic. Everyone loves it and everyone will eat it without fail, regardless of diet requirements, finicky moods, temper tantrums, and the like. Daniel, who is a distance runner, calls it rocket fuel when he eats a big bowl for breakfast right before a race. And even on the most terrible day of her terrible twos, Dahlia always consented to at least a few mouthfuls. As for me, well, I just like it, and am ever glad to brew up a batch.

I particularly like the way the coconut milk's creaminess softens the deep, toasty flavor of brown rice, but you can also make this with white rice; just reduce the cooking time to 20 minutes and cut back on the water you're adding (a scant 2 cups works well). The peas are strictly optional, but I like the bit of color they add, especially if you are serving this with the very brown Coconut Braised Beef on page 137. In that case, adding a small piece of cinnamon stick, about 1½ inches, to the pot offers up a warm scent that pairs beautifully with the exotic flavors of the beef.

serves 4

1 (13.5-ounce) can coconut milk

1 cup brown rice, rinsed

Large pinch kosher salt

¾ cup frozen peas (optional)

1. Pour the coconut milk into a liquid measuring cup. Add enough water to make 2 cups and pour the mixture into a large saucepan with the rice. Bring the liquid just to a boil and add the salt.

2. Reduce the heat to low, cover, and simmer until the liquid has been absorbed and the rice is tender, 45 minutes to 1 hour. Stir in the peas (if using) during the last 2 minutes of cooking. If the rice is tender but there is still liquid in the pan, remove the cover and cook over high heat until the liquid has evaporated. Fluff well before serving.

Rich and nutty brown butter corn bread with fresh corn

Here is something excellent to do with brown butter and corn.

This recipe started out as an accident. I was melting butter in a skillet while making corn bread and got distracted. When I came back to the stove, the butter was nut brown and fragrant instead of merely liquid, and made one of the richest, most deeply flavored corn breads I'd ever had.

Now it's my go-to corn bread recipe, and it's extremely adaptable. This version has sweet, nubby fresh corn kernels caramelized with the butter and maple syrup, but you can leave them out.

I've also added shredded or crumbled cheeses of all milks, chopped fresh herbs, chili powder, sautéed onions, diced jalapeño, minced roasted bell pepper, and shredded coconut. All work perfectly, though the corn bread doesn't really need them. The caramelized, buttery flavor can stand alone.

In a perfect world, try to time this so you can serve it warm from the oven. But you can also just heat it up by toasting slices before serving. More butter slathered on top doesn't hurt, either.

makes 1 (9-inch) corn bread; serves 6

½ cup (1 stick) unsalted butter

Kernels from 1 ear corn (about 1 cup; optional)

1 tablespoon pure maple syrup

1 cup all-purpose flour

1 cup stone-ground yellow cornmeal

1 tablespoon baking powder

¾ teaspoon kosher salt

1¼ cups plain full-fat yogurt or sour cream

1 large egg

2 tablespoons sugar

¼ teaspoon baking soda

1. Preheat the oven to 375°F.

2. In a 9-inch oven-safe skillet over medium-high heat, melt 4 tablespoons of the butter. Add the corn and maple syrup and sauté, stirring, until the corn is tender, 10 to 12 minutes. (If not using the corn, just melt together the butter and maple syrup.)

(continued)

3. In a large bowl, sift together the flour, cornmeal, baking powder, and salt. In a separate bowl, whisk together the yogurt, egg, sugar, and baking soda. Gently fold the wet ingredients into the dry ones until just combined. Fold in the corn-butter mixture.

4. Return the skillet to the heat and melt the remaining 4 tablespoons butter, tilting the pan to coat the sides completely. Cook the butter for 2 to 3 minutes, until pale gold with a nutty fragrance, being careful not to let it get too brown. Take the skillet off the heat and scrape in the batter, smoothing the surface with a rubber spatula.

5. Bake the corn bread until the top is golden and a toothpick inserted into the center comes out clean, 25 to 30 minutes. Cut into wedges and serve.

Barley with carrots, scallions, and maybe Parmesan

Cooking shredded carrots along with soft, nubby barley grains is a great way to get your toddler to eat vegetables. Or at least it was a relatively reliable way to get my toddler to do so. Of course when it comes to feeding two-year-olds, it's always a gamble. In any case, Daniel and I dependably like the gentle, moist barley seasoned with sharp spring scallions and plenty of good olive oil. So even if Dahlia turned up her nose, this dish found a welcoming plate.

It's good with hearty braised meats such as pork chops or any kind of flesh you've got stewing. And I also like it very much with crisp-skinned broiled or roasted chicken. Sometimes I stir in a pasted garlic clove to give this more oomph. For the adults, it's also good served with a squirt of Sriracha or other hot sauce, though what isn't?

serves 2 to 4

¼ teaspoon kosher salt, plus more for the cooking water

1 cup pearl barley

2 medium carrots, grated

⅓ cup finely grated Parmesan cheese (optional)

2 tablespoons extra-virgin olive oil

2 scallions, white and light green parts only, thinly sliced

¼ teaspoon freshly ground black pepper

1. Bring a large pot of salted water to a boil. Add the barley; reduce the heat to low, cover, and simmer until almost tender, 50 to 60 minutes. (If the water level gets too low before the barley is done, you can add more hot water as needed.) Stir in the carrots and cook until the carrots are tender and the grains are completely cooked, 5 to 10 minutes more.

2. Drain well and transfer the mixture to a large bowl. Stir in the Parmesan (if using), oil, scallions, salt, and pepper; serve warm.

Bulgur "pilaf" with Swiss chard and dried apricots

Daniel and I spent our honeymoon in Istanbul, a magical city with heavenly food. One of the most distinct and memorable dishes was one we sampled at the house of a friend of a friend. Engin Akin, an expert on Ottoman palace cuisine and a crackerjack cook, invited us over for a historic meal inspired by what the sultans ate during Ottoman times.

I was expecting to be awed by the food, but I did not expect my favorite dish to be a humble bulgur pilaf. It looked plain and brown, but the flavors exploded on my tongue—hints of cinnamon, allspice, and plenty of butter. It was so good that I immediately understood why a sultan who could command dishes from anywhere in his far-flung empire would insist on bulgur.

This pilaf is inspired by those fragrant yet homey flavors. However, instead of cooking the bulgur traditionally with sautéed onions and stock, I cook it in plenty of water, like pasta, which lets me simmer it until the grains are just tender, and I don't have to worry about getting the amount of liquid perfect.

After cooking, I added the spices and butter and some tender shoots of Swiss chard to give the dish some color and a vegetable quotient, along with dried apricots for sweetness and pistachios for crunch. Overall it's a heartier, more filling, and less nuanced dish than the one Ms. Akin served me, but no less compelling for its lack of authenticity.

serves 4

½ teaspoon kosher salt, plus more for the cooking water

1 cup medium- or coarse-ground bulgur

1 cinnamon stick

½ cup dried apricots, cut into ¼-inch cubes

1½ tablespoons unsalted butter

½ cup coarsely chopped raw pistachios

¾ teaspoon ground cumin

1 tablespoon extra-virgin olive oil

2 garlic cloves, finely chopped

1 shallot, finely chopped

1 bunch Swiss chard, stems removed and leaves chopped

¼ teaspoon freshly ground black pepper

Freshly squeezed lemon juice or pomegranate molasses, for drizzling

1. Bring a large pot of salted water to a boil. Add the bulgur and cinnamon stick; cook for about 9 minutes. Stir in the apricots and cook for 2 to 3 minutes more, or until the bulgur is tender (this might vary depending on how coarse the bulgur is). Drain well and discard the cinnamon stick.

2. In a large skillet over medium-high heat, melt the butter. Add the pistachios, cumin, and ¼ teaspoon of the salt. Cook, stirring, until golden, about 2 minutes. Transfer to a bowl.

3. Wipe out the skillet with a paper towel. Return it to medium heat and add the oil, garlic, and shallot. Cook, stirring, until the garlic is fragrant, about 30 seconds. Add the chard, remaining ¼ teaspoon salt, and the pepper. Cook, tossing, until the chard is wilted, about 3 minutes. Stir in the bulgur mixture and pistachios. Toss over the heat for 1 minute, until warmed through. Transfer to serving plates and drizzle with lemon juice or pomegranate molasses.

Roasted acorn squash, honey, smoked paprika, and sage salt

Seasoned salts—made from all manner of herbs, spices, and even nuts and meats—are all the rage. And while I've been lured into purchasing some of them, I can never seem to remember to use them.

Not so this woodsy-flavored sage salt. One day, faced with a surplus of sage from the pot on the deck, which needed to get used before it succumbed to a hard winter freeze, I made up a batch. Instead of banishing it to the nether regions of the spice drawer, I left it on the counter in a little bowl, then proceeded to sprinkle it on anything that needed a touch of salt.

And in my kitchen, that's a lot of things. I used it on eggs, soups, Chili (page 116), salads, even over slices of hot buttered whole-grain toast.

But the best dish I made with the salt was hands down this simple roasted acorn squash, which I also tossed with honey and smoked paprika for depth and sweetness. It would make a great Thanksgiving side dish if you doubled or tripled the recipe, and it's just as good at room temperature as it is hot (important if you're making it for Thanksgiving).

And if you don't want to make the sage salt yourself, you could probably even top the squash with one of those purchased salt blends you've probably been tempted into buying. It happens to the best of us.

serves 4 to 6

2 medium acorn squash, trimmed

2 tablespoons extra-virgin olive oil

2 teaspoons honey

1 teaspoon smoked sweet paprika

½ teaspoon kosher salt

4 large sage sprigs (about 16 nice leaves)

2 teaspoons coarse sea salt

1. Preheat the oven to 350°F.

2. Slice the squash crosswise into ½-inch rings. Use a spoon to scoop the seeds from the center of each ring; discard or reserve for toasting and snacking.

3. In a small bowl, whisk together the oil, honey, paprika, and kosher salt. Arrange the squash on a large baking sheet; pour the paprika oil over the squash, and toss well to combine. Place the sage leaves in a small baking pan.

(continued)

4. Transfer both pans to the oven. Roast the sage leaves until just crisp, about 10 minutes; transfer to a rack to cool. Increase the oven temperature to 400°F and continue roasting the squash, turning once, until tender and light golden, 20 to 25 minutes.

5. Transfer the squash to a platter. Crumble the sage in a small bowl (you should have about 1½ teaspoons) with the coarse salt; sprinkle some of the sage salt over the squash and serve.

Crushed new potatoes and pea salad with mustard seed dressing

I'd been cooking with and eating new potatoes for years before I finally learned that, in fact, I had not. Those cute little red potatoes I'd always called "new red potatoes"? Turns out they are not necessarily new at all.

My education came—where else?—at the farmers' market, when Franca Tantillo at Berried Treasures Farm proudly showed off a basket of her newly dug potatoes. She explained that potatoes are such good storing vegetables that they will last the whole winter through, so no one makes a tomato-like fuss when the freshly dug ones hit the farm stands along with the peas in early summer.

And do you know what? New potatoes, with their gossamer-thin skins and moist, almost nutty-tasting flesh, really are different—and better—than old potatoes. They have a rich, buttery flavor that needs just a touch of butter and salt to make a memorable side dish all by themselves.

But if you want something with a little more pizzazz, try this savory salad. It's got a little bit of a lot of different elements, and they all work together to enhance the gentle earthy character of the actually new potatoes, with peas adding a sweet crispness, yogurt lending tanginess, and Dijon mustard and mustard seeds spicing everything up with their warm bite. If you've only got old potatoes to cook with, make this anyway. Then follow Ms. Tantillo's advice and watch for new potatoes when they next come into season. And spread the word; they deserve a bit of fuss.

serves 4

1 pound new potatoes

½ teaspoon kosher salt, plus more for the cooking water

¾ cup shelled fresh peas

¾ teaspoon black or brown mustard seeds

3 tablespoons plain yogurt (optional)

2 teaspoons Dijon mustard

2 tablespoons finely chopped shallot

¼ teaspoon freshly ground black pepper

1 to 3 tablespoons extra-virgin olive oil, to taste

2 tablespoons chopped fresh mint or chives

(continued)

1. Place the potatoes in a large pot of salted water. Bring to a boil and cook until almost tender, about 20 minutes. Drop in the peas and cook until they are tender, 3 to 5 minutes. Drain well. Place the warm potatoes and peas in a large bowl and gently crush the potatoes (they should remain almost whole).

2. While the potatoes are cooking, in a small, dry skillet, toast the mustard seeds until they just begin to pop, about 1 minute. Transfer to a small bowl. Whisk in the yogurt (if using), Dijon mustard, shallot, salt, and pepper. Add the dressing and olive oil to the bowl with the potatoes and peas and toss to combine. Fold in the mint or chives. Taste and adjust the seasoning, if necessary. Serve warm.

Golden parsnip latkes

Shredded parsnip makes these crispy pancakes sweeter than the usual potato latkes, and the parsnips' dry flesh renders them extraordinarily crunchy, too.

I came up with the recipe during a brief period of parsnip experimentation, after I brought home a huge bag of the pale roots without any kind of plan about how to use them. Some found their way into a comforting, pureed soup (page 49), some I roasted simply with olive oil and salt, and the remainder got shredded and fried into latkes during one of the nights of Hanukkah, though I can't remember which. I do remember Daniel's and Dahlia's reactions to the brittle-textured, sweet-and-salty morsels. Not that they said much; they were too busy chewing. But gobbling speaks louder than words.

You can garnish these with all the usual potato pancake toppers, including sour cream and applesauce, but they are also wonderful plain, sprinkled with a little more salt.

makes about 18 latkes

1 pound parsnips (about 3 medium), halved crosswise

1 medium onion, quartered

½ cup all-purpose flour

2 large eggs

2½ teaspoons kosher salt

1 teaspoon baking powder

½ teaspoon freshly ground black pepper

Chicken fat, duck fat, or olive oil, for frying

1. Using a food processor with a coarse grating disc, grate the parsnips and onion. Transfer the mixture to a clean dishtowel and squeeze and wring out as much of the liquid as possible.

2. Working quickly, transfer the mixture to a large bowl. Add the flour, eggs, salt, baking powder, and pepper and mix until the flour has been absorbed.

3. In a heavy-bottomed medium pan over medium-high heat, heat about ¼ inch of chicken fat. Once the fat is hot (a drop of batter placed in the pan should sizzle), use a heaping tablespoon to drop the batter into the hot pan, cooking 3 or 4 latkes at one time. Use a spatula to flatten and shape the drops into discs. When the edges of the latkes are brown and crispy, 2 to 3 minutes, flip and cook until the second side is deeply browned, 2 to 3 minutes more. Transfer the latkes to a paper towel–lined plate to drain. Repeat with the remaining batter.

Creamy leek gratin with Parmesan

For years, I thought those first, fat leeks to hit the farmers' market in April were newly grown spring leeks. It never occurred to me that they were actually left over from last year's crop. The farmers set aside a patch of leeks, cover them thickly with hay, and let them hibernate in the freezing ground all winter long, plucking them when the thaw comes. Wintered-over leeks get very sweet from this treatment, which is odd since I know I'd get very grumpy if you tried to do the same thing to me.

Leeks vinaigrette is usually my go-to dish when I want super-sweet, wintered-over leeks to star. But I also adore the amazing, gooey, creamy leek gratin I've sampled over at Franny's restaurant near my home. The former sous-chef, Danny Amend, roasts the leeks in the wood oven before layering them into a casserole with heavy cream and cheese.

My version is streamlined and a bit lighter. I cut the cream with chicken broth and reduce the overall amount of cheese. It's rich without being heavy, and the leeks become wonderfully silky and deeply flavored as they slacken amid all the bubbling cream, butter, and broth, crowned with a golden and crisp cheese topping.

It makes a lovely side dish for something simple, maybe roasted chicken or broiled steak. Or pile it on toasted multigrain bread, as I have, for an odd but thoroughly satisfying dinner for one.

serves 4 to 6

¼ teaspoon kosher salt, plus more for the cooking water

2 pounds leeks (4 or 5 medium), white and light green parts only, trimmed and halved lengthwise

1 cup chicken broth or vegetable broth, plus more as needed

1 cup half-and-half or whole milk, plus more as needed

3 tablespoons unsalted butter

3 tablespoons all-purpose flour

⅛ teaspoon freshly ground black pepper

Pinch freshly grated nutmeg

Small pinch cayenne

8 ounces Gruyère cheese, grated (about 2 cups)

2 ounces Parmesan cheese, grated (about ½ cup)

1. Preheat the oven to 400°F. Lightly grease a 9 × 13-inch baking pan. Bring a large pot of salted water to a boil.

2. Run the leeks under cool water to remove any grit between the layers. Cook the leeks in the boiling water until almost tender, about 10 minutes. Drain well and pat completely dry.

3. In a small saucepan, warm the broth and half-and-half.

4. In a separate saucepan over medium-high heat, melt the butter. Add the flour and cook, stirring, until the roux is pale yellow and frothy, about 1 minute. Slowly whisk in the warm milk mixture and stir until thickened, 2 to 3 minutes. Reduce the heat to maintain a simmer and season with the salt, pepper, nutmeg, and cayenne; simmer for 1 minute more. Whisk in the Gruyère until melted. If the mixture seems too thick, thin it slightly with milk or a little broth.

5. Transfer the leeks, cut-side up, to the prepared pan. Spoon the sauce over the leeks. Sprinkle the top with the Parmesan. Bake until the sauce is bubbling and golden, about 40 minutes.

Hello, salad

TENDER GREENS WITH HERBS AND HAZELNUTS

If there was ever a culinary low point in my life, it was when, at the knowing age of about twenty-five, I decided I was giving up salad. The truth of it was that for much of my early, fat-phobic adulthood, I nearly subsisted on the stuff, dutifully chomping my way through vast mounds of slightly wilted, prewashed mesclun coated in a nonfat, Caesar-like dressing. It almost ruined my taste for the stuff. Thankfully, after a few months, I began to miss salad. So I started experimenting with vegetables and greens other than lettuce.

A bowl of watercress and slivered red peppers tossed with shredded Cheddar cheese and drizzled with olive oil? Now, *that* makes a tasty lunch. Shredded carrots slathered with mayonnaise and orange juice is delightfully satisfying. And there is nothing heinous about baby arugula at all, especially when dressed with walnut oil and a few drops of my mother's homemade vinegar. Little by little, I made my way back to salad, though I admit that I still won't go near bagged mesclun or nonfat dressing of any kind.

Now no dinner is complete without a big bowl of some kind of crisp greens gracing the table. And when I serve it to my husband, Daniel, he greets it like a long-lost friend, even though we eat salad every night.

"Hello, salad," he says affectionately, piling his plate high.

serves 2 to 4

1 teaspoon sherry vinegar, white wine vinegar, or champagne vinegar	6 cups loosely packed tender baby greens
⅛ teaspoon kosher salt, plus more to taste	Handful mixed fresh soft herbs, such as cilantro, mint, parsley, and/or basil
1½ tablespoons hazelnut or walnut oil	¼ cup chopped toasted hazelnuts or walnuts (see Note)

1. Combine the vinegar and salt in a small bowl and mix well to dissolve the salt. Slowly whisk in the oil.

2. Place the greens, herbs, and hazelnuts or walnuts in a large bowl and toss with the vinaigrette. Season with more salt to taste.

   note: To toast nuts, spread them on a baking sheet and bake at 325°F, stirring every 5 minutes, until they start to smell nutty, 10 to 20 minutes depending on the type and size of the nut. Cool completely before chopping.

Southeast Asian tomato salad

I tossed this together one night to serve with the Thai-style Ground Turkey dish (page 114). It's a departure from my usual tomato salad, which is composed of little more than carved-up tomatoes, torn basil, salt, and olive oil. Daniel and I eat this simple salad almost every night in tomato season, since it takes about twenty seconds to assemble and has a juicy purity of tomato flavor that I can't seem to get enough of this time of year.

But with the fish sauce, limes, scallions, and jalapeños for the turkey already sitting out within arm's reach, I decided to try something new.

It turned out to be insanely good, very tangy, and a nice break from the more everyday, if tasty, tomato salads I usually make. I've since added it to our summer tomato rotation (sometimes with a sliced Kirby cucumber standing in for one of the tomatoes) and find myself whipping it up even if I have to hunt in the cupboard for the fish sauce and sort through the vegetable bin for a jalapeño. It's worth the chase every time.

serves 4

About 2 teaspoons Asian fish sauce, such as nam pla or nuoc mam, or to taste

2 teaspoons freshly squeezed lime juice

1 teaspoon light brown sugar

2 scallions, finely chopped

1 fat garlic clove, minced (or use 2 small ones)

½ jalapeño, seeded, if desired, and finely chopped

3 large or 4 medium tomatoes, sliced ¼ inch thick

2 tablespoons chopped fresh Thai or regular basil

2 tablespoons chopped fresh cilantro

1. In a small bowl, whisk together the fish sauce, lime juice, brown sugar, scallions, garlic, and jalapeño. (If you think your fish sauce is very salty, start with 1 teaspoon; you can add more at the end.)

2. Arrange the tomato slices on a plate. Spoon the dressing over the tomatoes. Let stand for 10 minutes to allow the tomatoes time to release their juices. Sprinkle with the basil and cilantro; serve.

Celery salad with walnuts and Parmesan

When there's nothing else in the house to make into salad, I remember the celery.

It's always there when I need it to be, a neglected stalwart usually just waiting to be mixed up with tuna and mayo or sautéed into a soup. Sometimes I'll forget about it for weeks. But then, when I'm craving a salad and the greens in the fridge are sad and wilted, I'll slice up some crisp celery stalks, toss them with a little olive oil and lemon juice, and enjoy a quickly made, always available salad with a juicy fresh bite.

If I've got them on hand, sometimes I'll sprinkle a few walnuts into the salad bowl. The nuts add a different kind of crunch—a softer, buttery, rich crunch against the celery's watery, cold, snappy crunch. The two together are compelling, especially when topped with some shaved good Parmesan cheese to add a salty creaminess to the mix (but any aged cheese, such as Cheddar, Gouda, or Manchego, can stand in nicely). I'll eat it all up, and think, *Why don't I make this more often?* It makes me happy every time.

serves 4

1 cup walnuts

1½ tablespoons red wine vinegar

½ teaspoon kosher salt

Freshly ground black pepper, to taste

⅓ cup extra-virgin olive oil

8 large celery stalks, with leaves, thinly sliced

2 ounces good Parmesan cheese, shaved

1. Preheat the oven to 350°F.

2. Spread the walnuts in a single layer on a rimmed baking sheet. Toast in the oven, tossing once halfway through, until the nuts are golden, 7 to 10 minutes. Let cool and coarsely chop.

3. In a small bowl, whisk together the vinegar, salt, and pepper to taste; whisk in the oil. Combine the walnuts, celery and leaves, and cheese in a large salad bowl. Add the vinaigrette and toss gently to combine.

Garlicky sesame-cured broccoli salad

After years of rejection on the potluck circuit, one of my favorite dishes—marinated raw broccoli salad—was overdue for a rechristening.

It's made from uncooked broccoli tossed with an assertive garlic, sesame, chile, and cumin seed vinaigrette slicked with good extra-virgin olive oil and red wine vinegar. The acid "cooks" the florets a little, like ceviche. After an hour, the broccoli softens as if blanched, turning bright emerald and soaking up all the intense flavors of the dressing. Fresh, crunchy, and deeply garlicky, it's easily the most addictive vegetable in my repertory. Plus, I can make it in minutes and it keeps for days, becoming even tangier as it sits. I've even increased the dressing and added cubed tofu or cooked shrimp to turn the salad into a main course. But marinated raw broccoli salad, as a name, just didn't resonate with people.

So the next time I was invited to a potluck, I unveiled a shiny new title that highlighted the broccoli's best attributes: Garlicky Sesame-Cured Broccoli Salad.

Later that night, I overheard two guests talking about it.

"I don't know what it's called," one of them said, "but it's terrific."

And that was just fine by me.

serves 6 to 8 as a side dish, or more as an hors d'oeuvre

1½ teaspoons red wine vinegar

1 teaspoon kosher salt, plus more to taste

2 heads broccoli (1 pound each), cut into bite-size florets

¾ cup extra-virgin olive oil

4 fat garlic cloves, minced

2 teaspoons cumin seeds

2 teaspoons toasted (Asian) sesame oil

Large pinch crushed red pepper flakes

1. In a large, heat-proof bowl, stir together the vinegar and salt. Add the broccoli and toss to combine.

2. In a large skillet over medium-high heat, heat the olive oil until hot but not smoking. Add the garlic and cumin and cook until fragrant, about 1 minute. Stir in the sesame oil and red pepper flakes. Pour the mixture over the broccoli and toss well. Let sit for at least 1 hour at room temperature, or refrigerate for up to 48 hours (chill it if you want to keep it for more than 2 hours). Taste and adjust the seasonings (it may need more salt); serve.

Honey-roasted carrot salad with arugula and almonds

The sweetest little carrots start appearing in the farmers' market in June, and I have a particular affection for the thumb-size, pale-orange roots. They remind me of those few childhood years when my parents gave over nearly the entirety of our 0.6-acre Brooklyn backyard to cultivate a vegetable garden.

Most of it never ripened (the corn was really pushing it). But just like in the classic children's book *The Carrot Seed*, the carrots did come up. We pulled them from the ground while they were still in their infancy, and ate them rinsed under the garden hose, still warm from the ground.

And even if the ones from the farmers' market aren't quite as sweet as those home-grown carrots from summertimes past, I can use them to make something good to eat, like this lovely, mellow salad. Roasting the carrots condenses their gentle flavor, making them rich and caramelized, a process I encourage by brushing them with a little honey. When they are soft and browned, I toss them with almonds for crunch and arugula for a pleasing bitter contrast. I won't wax poetic and pretend that a bite of my roasted carrot salad brings me back to my childhood, standing in the garden in muddy sneakers, carrots in hand. No, that moment is for that one-in-a-hundred carrot that happens maybe every few years.

But my ongoing search means that I get to eat a lot of carrot salads, and this is easily one of the best.

serves 4

FOR THE SALAD

1 pound carrots (about 5 medium), cut into ½-inch rounds

1½ tablespoons plus 2 teaspoons extra-virgin olive oil

½ teaspoon plus 1 large pinch kosher salt

¼ teaspoon freshly ground black pepper

2 teaspoons honey

¼ cup sliced almonds

2 bunches arugula (about 8 cups)

FOR THE VINAIGRETTE

1½ teaspoons freshly squeezed lemon juice

½ teaspoon kosher salt

½ teaspoon freshly ground black pepper

¼ cup extra-virgin olive oil

(continued)

1. MAKE THE SALAD: Preheat the oven to 400°F.

2. In a large bowl, toss together the carrots, 1½ tablespoons of the oil, ½ teaspoon of the salt, and the pepper. Spread the carrots in an even layer on a large baking sheet. Roast, stirring occasionally, for 25 minutes.

3. Meanwhile, in a small bowl, whisk together the honey, the remaining 2 teaspoons oil, 1 teaspoon water, and the remaining pinch of salt. Toss the almonds with 1½ teaspoons of the honey mixture and spread them on a small baking sheet.

4. Transfer the almonds to the oven; at the same time, pour the remaining honey mixture over the carrots. Roast until the carrots are tender and caramelized and the nuts are dark golden, 5 to 7 minutes. Let the nuts and carrots cool completely.

5. MAKE THE VINAIGRETTE: In a small bowl, whisk together the lemon juice, salt, and pepper. Whisk in the oil until incorporated.

6. In a large bowl, toss together the arugula, carrots, and almonds. Add the vinaigrette and toss well to combine.

Winter salad with fennel, radicchio, walnuts, and Manchego

When the weather turns cold and all the tender salad greens start to look as if they've seen better days, I know I can reach for radicchio and it won't let me down. With the bright-hued look of an overgrown Christmas tree ornament, the tightly coiled magenta leaves unfurl once sliced, blossoming onto the cutting board in a florid heap. One snowball-size head will fill a salad bowl for four, especially when augmented with thinly sliced fennel and garnished with crunchy nuts and salty, creamy cheese.

Radicchio is a bitter lettuce. I find that the sweetness of the fennel is enough to temper it for my taste, but you can add a handful of raisins or chopped dates if you find you need more. Or instead, substitute two or three Belgium endives for the radicchio; it will be beautifully pale with a delicate, sweet character.

No matter what, it's a filling salad that makes a fine lunch on its own. Or serve it as the first course to an elegant dinner.

serves 4

1½ tablespoons freshly squeezed lemon juice

½ teaspoon kosher salt

½ teaspoon freshly ground black pepper

1 fat garlic clove, finely chopped

¼ cup extra-virgin olive oil

4 ounces aged Manchego or Parmesan cheese

⅓ cup walnuts, toasted (see page 160) and finely chopped

1 large head radicchio, quartered lengthwise and cored

1 large fennel bulb, fronds chopped and reserved

1. In a bowl, whisk together the lemon juice, salt, pepper, and garlic. Whisk in the oil. Use a Microplane or other grater to finely grate 2 ounces of the cheese (you'll get about ½ cup). Whisk the grated cheese and walnuts into the vinaigrette (it should be fairly thick).

2. Thinly slice each radicchio wedge crosswise and transfer to a large salad bowl. Trim the stems from the fennel and remove the outer layers. Cut the fennel bulb in half from top to bottom. Using a mandoline or very sharp knife, shave the fennel into paper-thin slices. Add to the salad bowl.

3. Pour the vinaigrette over the salad and toss well. Use a vegetable peeler to shave the remaining 2 ounces of cheese into curls. Toss into the salad. Taste and adjust the seasonings, if necessary. Garnish with the fennel fronds, if desired.

Zucchini with mint and garlic

As part of the copious antipasti selection that always preceded the belt-unbuckling, multicourse, Italian American feasts she modestly referred to as "Sunday dinner," zucchini with mint and garlic was one of my favorite dishes that my ex-mother-in-law made.

She'd hunch over the kitchen table, thinly slicing the daintiest of zucchini by hand with her favorite blunt little paring knife, despite the fact that my father-in-law kept dozens of freshly sharpened knives in the drawer. Then she'd sear the zucchini on her grill pan, turning the neat slices over and over until they were soft and browned, drizzling them with a little olive oil, then scattering the cooked ones with pungent minced garlic and fresh chopped mint.

She would serve them along with the things she brought in from Arthur Avenue—the soft and milky mozzarella that had never seen a refrigerator, loaves of crunchy semolina bread, bright green cured olives, and special aged pork sausage. There were other homemade vegetables, too: Fat bell peppers, roasted, peeled, and marinated in red wine vinegar. Sweet-and-sour eggplant salad with capers. Sweet pickled carrots with chopped parsley. She and my father-in-law ate the leftovers all week long.

Of all her recipes, the zucchini is the one I make most often. Instead of a grill pan, I use the broiler. Then I serve it cold or warm, usually as a side dish to a meal that is, sadly, not as bountiful as at my ex-mother-in-law's.

serves 4

1¼ pounds zucchini (about 4 small), sliced ⅛ inch thick

2 tablespoons extra-virgin olive oil, plus more for drizzling

¾ teaspoon kosher salt, plus more to taste

1 garlic clove, minced

1 tablespoon chopped fresh mint or basil

1. Preheat the broiler.

2. In a bowl, toss the zucchini with the oil and salt. Arrange the slices on two baking sheets in an even layer.

3. Broil until the slices begin to brown, about 5 minutes. Flip the slices and broil for about 5 minutes more. Transfer the zucchini to a bowl and toss with the garlic and mint. Drizzle with additional oil and season with salt to taste.

Garlicky broccoli rabe

Hearty pasta and risotto dishes need bright, zesty, green-vegetable side dishes to wake up all that sleepy, starchy comfort food. Sautéed bitter broccoli rabe is one of my favorites. It's simple and very tasty, and I make it all the time in the colder months. That's when all the best crucifers are in season, and when I tend to crave the deep, sharp flavor of bitter greens tamed with plenty of garlic and chile. Regular broccoli, Broccolini, kale, or fresh spinach take well to the same combination.

I've seen many recipes that call for blanching the broccoli rabe before sautéing it. I've never found that necessary. Covering the pan after sautéing will steam-cook it without the need for another pot to wash, because, really, who wants to deal with more dishes?

Sometimes, when I'm home alone and not in the mood for a full-on meal (maybe I've had a big restaurant lunch or ate too many cookies in the afternoon), I'll make this for dinner and serve it on its own. It's so satisfying that I don't miss the pasta or polenta or chicken or whatever usually goes with it. And one large, fluffy bunch of broccoli rabe perfectly feeds one (this one, anyway) for a spunky solo dinner.

serves 1 or 2

2 tablespoons extra-virgin olive oil

2 fat garlic cloves, finely chopped

Large pinch crushed red pepper flakes

1 large bunch broccoli rabe, tough stems removed

¾ teaspoon kosher salt

In a skillet over medium heat, heat the oil until hot. Add the garlic and red pepper flakes; cook until fragrant, about 30 seconds. Add the broccoli rabe and salt and toss well. Cook for 1 minute. Stir in 2 tablespoons water. Cover the pan and cook until tender, 3 to 4 minutes. If necessary, cook, uncovered, to evaporate any excess water in the pan.

Shredded Brussels sprouts with pancetta and caraway

For years, my preferred way to eat Brussels sprouts was halved and roasted until the outer leaves got crisp and dark brown, while the centers softened and mellowed. The recipe was almost too easy. I just tossed the halved sprouts with olive oil and salt, roasted them at high heat, and then ate them by the bowlful.

Then I met a whole other kind of Brussels sprout dish. Instead of halved, these sprouts were shredded, then quickly sautéed over high heat so the edges turned golden. Compared to the halved sprouts, there was more browning, which meant more caramelization and a sweeter flavor. But another thing I liked was the way the shreds absorbed all the good seasonings in the pan, which never quite penetrate the dense halved sprouts in the same way.

When I made my own shredded sprouts a few weeks later, I looked toward Northern Europe for inspiration. I started with pancetta, crisping it in the pan and rendering out fat to coat the shreds. I hoped its gentle, porky flavor would bring out the sweetness of the sprouts. I also added a pinch of caraway seeds to the pan because the pile of shredded sprouts in my food processor looked a little like green cabbage, and green cabbage reminds me of Germany, and Germany reminds me of caraway.

The final sprouts were pure bliss—tender, crisp-edged, pork-coated, and garlicky—and well worth the deviation.

serves 6

1 pound Brussels sprouts	4 ounces pancetta, diced small (½ cup)
3 tablespoons extra-virgin olive oil	½ teaspoon kosher salt
4 garlic cloves, finely chopped	Freshly ground black pepper, to taste
1½ teaspoons caraway seeds	

1. Use a paring knife to trim the bottoms of the sprouts; peel away any browned leaves. In a food processor fitted with the slicing blade, shred the Brussels sprouts. Toss the sprouts with 2 tablespoons of the oil, the garlic, and the caraway seeds.

2. In a large skillet over medium-high heat, heat the remaining 1 tablespoon oil. Add the pancetta and cook until golden, 3 to 5 minutes. Add the Brussels sprout mixture and cook, tossing, until wilted, 1 to 2 minutes. Season with the salt and pepper to taste.

Wilted collard greens with lemon and extra-virgin olive oil

This is collard greens in their most pure and delicate manifestation, without ham hocks or hot sauce or chile or garlic to distract you from their sweet, grassy flavor. The greens are blanched in salted water, drained, and dressed simply, with olive oil, lemon juice, and salt—just enough to bring out their fresh taste without covering it up under the assumption that, in fact, you don't really like collard greens at all and you are just eating them for the meat and condiments they are cooked with.

If you meet this closet collard-hating criteria, this recipe isn't for you.

But if you love the taste of all things green, this will become a standard in your repertoire as it has in mine. I especially like to make it to accompany a highly seasoned stew or pasta dish; the mellowness acts as a great foil for spicy, intense flavors. However, if you eat the collards alone and find them on the bland side, no one is going to stop you from brandishing the hot sauce bottle or adding some crumbled feta and kalamatas to the bowl. The good thing about having your own kitchen, Julia Child supposedly said after she dropped a chicken on the floor, is that nobody can see what you are doing. Hail to that.

serves 2 to 4

Kosher salt, to taste

1 large bunch collard greens, stems removed and leaves torn into pieces

2 tablespoons good olive oil, plus more to taste

1 tablespoon freshly squeezed lemon juice, plus more to taste

1. Bring a large pot of salted water to a boil. Add the collard greens and let wilt. Cook until the leaves are soft enough to please you, 2 to 7 minutes depending on the age of the greens and your desire for tenderness.

2. Drain the collards and press out as much water as you can with a large spoon or a spatula. Put the greens in a bowl and toss with the oil, lemon juice, and salt to taste. Adjust the seasonings to taste.

Red chard with pine nuts, garlic, and golden rum raisins

This is one of those serendipitous dishes, a combination of ingredients that I wouldn't have ever thought to put together myself; but once I tasted the dish, it seemed inevitable.

It happened one Christmas Eve, when Daniel and I had a dinner party that was larger than usual, and I asked a friend of a friend, Amber Campion, to come help me with the cooking and cleanup.

I'd planned most of the menu ahead, but I bought several nice bunches of red chard, cleaned them, and put them next to the stove, figuring I'd sauté them with garlic and chile flakes at the last minute.

Then, with the party in full swing, I was too distracted to return to the stove. Amber offered to sauté them with pine nuts and raisins, one of her favorite dishes. It was so remarkably good that everyone asked Amber for the recipe, including me.

She explained what she did, and it sounded simple enough—but too simple for the nuanced flavors on our plates. There had to be some secret ingredient in that chard, and I got a little ticked off that she wasn't divulging it.

Finally, I realized what it was: aged dark rum. Amber had accidentally added a container of rum raisins I had made for some holiday baking but had never used. The rum added a mild smokiness and sweetness, which set off the slightly bitter chard to perfection. Now, even if I don't add raisins, I'll often splash a little dark rum into a pan of sautéed greens. It's my secret ingredient.

serves 8

¾ cup golden raisins

¼ cup dark rum

4 large bunches red chard

⅔ cup pine nuts

⅓ cup extra-virgin olive oil

2 large garlic cloves, finely chopped

¾ teaspoon kosher salt

¼ teaspoon freshly ground black pepper

1. In a small saucepan, combine the raisins, rum, and 2 tablespoons water. Simmer over medium-low heat until the raisins are plump and most of the liquid has evaporated, about 3 minutes.

2. Remove the center ribs from the chard and discard. Slice the leaves 1 inch wide. In your largest skillet over medium heat, toast the pine nuts, tossing occasionally, until golden, about 5 minutes. Transfer the nuts to a bowl.

3. In the same skillet over medium-high heat, heat the oil. Add the garlic and cook, stirring, until fragrant, about 30 seconds. Add the chard, a handful at a time, and cook until wilted, 6 to 8 minutes total. Season the greens with the salt and pepper. Stir the raisins and nuts into the skillet; toss to combine.

desserts

Upside-down polenta plum cake

There is cake served with fruit compote, and then there is upside-down cake. The two are similar on the surface—both consist of cakes topped with cooked sugared fruit—but the differences in texture and flavor are profound. Upside-down cake is better.

This is because spreading a layer of sweetened fruit beneath the batter accomplishes several delectable things. The compote continues to caramelize in the oven, turning butterscotchy, candied, and shiny, while delicately flavoring the cake batter through and through. Plus, in this particular example, the syrupy topping helps keep the cake moist for several days, while the cornmeal in the batter keeps everything from getting soggy.

Although you can probably use almost any fruit in this recipe, I like tangier, more acidic fruits best—think plums, rhubarb, raspberries, blackberries, cranberries, apricots, and the classic pineapple—to counter all the sugar you need to use to create a caramelized topping. If you would like to use low-acid fruit such as strawberries or pears, add a healthy squeeze of lemon or lime to the compote, along with grated zest.

I make a version of this rustic, coarse-crumbed upside-down cake all year long, varying the fruit to match what's around. But summer, when I always buy too much fruit to eat between market visits, is the ideal time. It's one of the few homey, not-too-sweet summer treats worth turning the oven on for. Even in August.

serves 8

1¾ pounds plums, rinsed, pitted, and sliced ½ inch thick

1½ cups plus 2 tablespoons sugar

¾ teaspoon kosher salt

1 cup fine cornmeal

½ cup all-purpose flour

1½ teaspoons baking powder

1 cup (2 sticks) unsalted butter, at room temperature

4 large eggs

⅓ cup sour cream or plain full-fat yogurt

2 teaspoons vanilla extract

Whipped cream or ice cream, for serving (optional)

1. Preheat the oven to 350°F. Line a 9-inch springform pan with parchment paper and grease the parchment and pan well.

2. In a large skillet over medium-high heat, cook the plums, ½ cup plus 2 tablespoons of the sugar, and ¼ teaspoon of the salt, stirring occasionally, until the plums are tender and the liquid begins to reduce, about 20 minutes. Spread the mixture into the prepared pan.

3. In a bowl, whisk together the cornmeal, flour, baking powder, and remaining ½ teaspoon salt.

4. In the bowl of an electric mixer fitted with the paddle attachment, cream the butter and the remaining 1 cup sugar until light and fluffy. Add the eggs one at a time and beat to combine. Beat in the sour cream and vanilla.

5. Use a spatula to fold in the dry ingredients. Scrape the batter over the plums and smooth with a spatula. Bake until the cake is golden and springs back when touched lightly, 45 to 55 minutes.

6. Allow the cake to cool in the pan for 10 minutes, then unmold the sides and invert onto a plate. Serve warm with whipped cream or ice cream, if desired.

Chocolate chip pecan loaf cake

One of my favorite wedding gifts is a whimsical, undulating porcelain cake stand with a domed glass cover. Presiding over the counter like an elegant dowager, its presence cajoles: "Isn't it time to make some lovely cake?"

For a cake enthusiast like myself, the answer is always yes, and I've been building up a small repertoire of quick, easy cakes that I can whip up without turning on (and later cleaning) the food processor or electric mixer.

The key is using liquid fat (melted butter or oil) that doesn't require creaming, and chemical leavening (baking powder and/or soda) to eliminate the vigorous beating of eggs.

This recipe is similar to a pound cake, with a sweet, buttery crumb that melds well with the pecans and chocolate—almost like a big, soft chocolate chip cookie in sliceable form. Using melted butter for the fat means the results aren't as light textured as oil-based cakes, but they do have a richer, more complex flavor.

Simple cakes like this have made it possible to keep my cake stand occupied for the better part of my marriage, and that, in turn, keeps everyone happy.

serves 8 to 10

1 cup sugar	¼ teaspoon baking soda
⅔ cup plain full-fat yogurt	¼ teaspoon kosher salt
3 large eggs	⅔ cup unsalted butter, melted
1¾ cups all-purpose flour	½ cup chocolate chips
1½ teaspoons baking powder	½ cup chopped toasted pecans

1. Preheat the oven to 350°F. Grease a 9 × 5-inch loaf pan.

2. In a large bowl, whisk together the sugar and yogurt. Add the eggs, one at a time, and whisk until completely combined.

3. In a separate bowl, mix together the flour, baking powder, baking soda, and salt. Add the dry mixture into the wet and mix until just combined.

4. Using a spatula, fold in the melted butter a little at a time. Fold in the chocolate chips and pecans.

5. Scrape the batter into the prepared pan and bake for 50 to 55 minutes, or until the cake is golden and a toothpick inserted into the center comes out clean. Allow the cake to cool in the pan for 5 minutes before turning it out onto a wire rack to cool to room temperature, right-side up.

Whiskey-soaked dark chocolate Bundt cake

My friend Dave is a cocktail fanatic, so a bourbon-imbued cake is just the thing to take to his birthday party. In particular, there's a boozy, fudge-filled 86-proof chocolate cake from *Maida Heatter's Book of Great Chocolate Desserts* that is so extravagant, it earned me temporary entry into my high school's cool clique when I first started making it, back when I was underage. I hadn't looked at the recipe in years, but there it was, the instructions splattered with chocolate smudges and my cryptic note in the margin to drizzle the cake with extra spirits.

I remembered the cake as delectable but slightly on the sweet side, with a flavor that spoke more of butter, liquor, and sugar than intense dark chocolate. So to deepen the flavor and cut the sweetness, I added a couple of tablespoons of unsweetened cocoa powder in addition to using a fancy-pants brand of requisite unsweetened chocolate, Valrhona. I also increased the amount of salt because I like my chocolate with a savory undertone.

Maida had also included a goodly half cup of bourbon in the batter. I planned to double that, replacing some of the water she called for. But because Dave espouses rye in Manhattans in lieu of bourbon, I thought maybe he'd like it in his birthday cake, too.

And, in fact, he did. The cake—rich, dense, and very chocolaty, with a spicy, peppery, burnt-caramel tang from the rye—was a hit. After all, who could resist raising a toast and a fork at the same time?

serves 10 to 12

5 ounces unsweetened chocolate

¼ cup instant espresso powder

2 tablespoons unsweetened cocoa powder

1 cup bourbon, rye, or other whiskey, plus more for sprinkling

½ teaspoon kosher salt

1 cup (2 sticks) unsalted butter, at room temperature

2 cups granulated sugar

3 large eggs

1 tablespoon vanilla extract

1 teaspoon baking soda

2 cups all-purpose flour, plus additional for the pan

Powdered cocoa or confectioners' sugar, for garnish (optional)

(continued)

FAVORITE RECIPES FROM MELISSA CLARK'S KITCHEN

1. Preheat the oven to 325°F. Grease and flour a 10-cup-capacity Bundt cake pan (or you can use two 8- or 9-inch loaf pans).

2. In the microwave or in the top of a double boiler over simmering water, melt the chocolate. Let cool.

3. Put the espresso and cocoa powder in a 2-cup (or larger) glass measuring cup. Add enough boiling water to come up to the 1-cup measuring line. Mix until the cocoa and espresso powders dissolve. Add the whiskey and salt; let cool.

4. In the bowl of an electric mixer fitted with the paddle attachment, beat the butter until fluffy. Add the granulated sugar and beat until well combined. Beat in the eggs, one at a time, beating well after each addition. Beat in the vanilla, baking soda, and melted chocolate, making sure to scrape down the sides of the bowl with a rubber spatula.

5. On low speed, beat in a third of the whiskey mixture. When the liquid has been absorbed, beat in half the flour. Repeat the additions, ending with the whiskey mixture. Scrape the batter into the prepared pan and smooth the top. Bake until a cake tester inserted into the center of the cake comes out clean, about 1 hour 10 minutes for the Bundt pan (the loaf pans will take less time; start checking them after 55 minutes).

6. Transfer the cake to a wire rack. Unmold after 15 minutes and sprinkle the warm cake with more whiskey. Let cool before serving, garnished with powdered cocoa or confectioners' sugar, if you like.

Tiny Valentine's day cake for Daniel

DEVIL'S FOOD CAKE WITH BUTTER RUM FROSTING

I acquired my first 6-inch cake pans when I made a wedding cake for two friends in graduate school. Let's just say that first cake was a good lesson in why professionally made cakes cost what they do. Luckily, it hardly mattered, as the bride and groom drank so many congratulatory shots that they barely noticed the cake, which the tipsy guests devoured with their hands when we ran out of forks.

Those pans have been put to good use ever since, and not just for wedding cakes. I also love using them to bake tiny layer cakes to feed four to six people. Or, for Valentine's Day, two, with ample leftovers for breakfast the next morning.

When making a meringue buttercream, pay attention to the temperature of the ingredients. The butter really needs to be soft, pliable, and at room temperature, not melty, not hard. So take it out of the fridge an hour before you plan to make this. The egg whites must be completely cool, not warm, when you add the butter. Basically, the butter and egg whites should be the same temperature. If one is too cold, the mixture will curdle; too hot, and it will melt into soup. If you do get soup, set the bowl briefly in a bowl of ice water, then try beating it again. If it's curdled, set the bowl in a bowl of very warm water and try beating it again. Fear not—broken buttercream can usually be rescued.

serves 4 to 6 (or 2 with leftovers)

FOR THE CHOCOLATE CAKE

⅔ cup very hot coffee or water

⅓ cup unsweetened Dutch-process cocoa powder

¾ teaspoon kosher salt

4 large egg yolks (save the whites for the buttercream)

1 tablespoon vanilla extract

1½ cups cake flour

2 teaspoons baking powder

½ cup (1 stick) unsalted butter, at room temperature

1 cup sugar

FOR THE BUTTER RUM FROSTING

4 large egg whites

1 cup sugar

¼ teaspoon kosher salt

1½ cups (3 sticks) unsalted butter, sliced, at room temperature

3 tablespoons good aged rum

1 cup chopped toasted pecans or purchased toffee bits (optional)

1. MAKE THE CAKE: Preheat the oven to 350°F. Grease and flour two 6-inch cake pans, or spray with baking spray. Cut parchment or waxed paper rounds to fit in the bottom of the pans, lay them down, and grease the paper.

2. In a small bowl, stir together the coffee and cocoa powder until smooth. Stir in the salt and let cool until barely warm to the touch. Whisk in the egg yolks and vanilla.

3. In a large bowl, whisk together the flour and baking powder.

4. In the bowl of an electric mixer fitted with the paddle attachment, beat the butter until fluffy. Add the sugar and beat until very light, about 5 minutes. Beat in a third of the cocoa mixture, followed by half the flour mixture, and beat well. Scrape down the sides of the bowl and beat again. Beat in another third of the cocoa mixture and then the remaining flour mixture. Scrape the sides again and add the remaining cocoa mixture. Beat until smooth.

5. Divide the batter evenly between the two cake pans and smooth the tops. Bake until the tops of the cakes are no longer shiny and wet looking, and a cake tester inserted into the center comes out clean, 30 to 35 minutes. Cool on wire racks before unmolding.

6. MEANWHILE, MAKE THE BUTTER RUM FROSTING: Put the egg whites, sugar, and salt into the clean metal bowl of your electric mixer (or any metal bowl, if using a handheld mixer). Bring a medium pot of water to a boil. Place the bowl of egg whites over the pot (make sure the bottom of the bowl does not touch the water) and whisk until the sugar has dissolved and the eggs are warm to the touch. Use pot holders if necessary to hold on to the bowl.

7. Remove the bowl from the heat and attach the bowl to your mixer. Beat the eggs with the whisk attachment until they are thick and cool, about 5 minutes. Beat in the butter, bit by bit, until the mixture is smooth and fluffy and buttercreamy. Beat in the rum. Use immediately, or store covered at room temperature for up to 24 hours. You might have to beat it again before using.

8. If the cakes are quite domed on top, use a knife to slice off the humps so the cake will be level (this is what professionals do to get perfectly even layers). Slice the cakes in half horizontally, and spread the buttercream between the layers, adding some of the chopped nuts or toffee bits if you like. Ice the cake, then cover with more of the nuts or toffee.

Blood orange olive oil cake

For quick loaf pan cakes like this, usually I rely on melted butter for the fat, with its richer flavor. But years ago, when our infant's diagnosis of gastroesophageal reflux disease led to the suggestion that I, her breast-feeding mama, give up cow's-milk dairy, I had to switch. As I read through recipes calling for vegetable oil, it occurred to me that my favorite vegetable oil is olive. So why not use that?

The recipe for Dorie Greenspan's extra-virgin olive oil cake seemed like just the place to start. And while I didn't have lime zest, I did have some nice blood oranges, so I grated the peel from those instead. That left me with two denuded oranges, which, I feared, would fossilize before I had a chance to eat them. A small wave of anticipatory guilt that I'd have to throw out fruit that cost $1.50 each made me decide to use them immediately. I juiced one and chopped up segments from the other, adding it all to the cake batter and reducing the quantity of yogurt (I used sheep's milk) to compensate for the extra liquid.

While the cake was baking, every corner of the house pulsed with the scents of citrus and olive. I could barely wait for my cake to cool before cutting a sliver. With a distinct herbal flavor from the oil and juicy bits of ruby blood orange strewn throughout the very fine crumb, it was both pretty and every bit as good as my more buttery confections.

serves 8 to 10

3 blood oranges	¼ teaspoon baking soda
1 cup sugar	¼ teaspoon fine sea salt
Buttermilk or plain yogurt, as needed	⅔ cup extra-virgin olive oil
3 large eggs	Whipped cream, for serving (optional)
1¾ cups all-purpose flour	Honey–Blood Orange Compote (see Note), for serving (optional)
1½ teaspoons baking powder	

1. Preheat the oven to 350°F. Grease a 9 × 5-inch loaf pan.

2. Grate the zest from 2 oranges and place in a bowl with the sugar. Using your fingers, rub the zest and sugar together until the orange zest is evenly distributed.

3. SUPRÊME ONE OF THE ORANGES: Cut off the bottom and top so the fruit is exposed and the orange can stand upright on a cutting board. Cut away the peel and pith, following the curve of the fruit with your knife. Cut the orange segments out of their connective membranes and let them fall into a bowl. Repeat with another orange. Break up the segments with your fingers.

(continued)

4. Halve the remaining orange and squeeze the juice into a measuring cup. You'll have ¼ cup or so. Add buttermilk or yogurt to the juice until you have ⅔ cup liquid altogether. Pour the mixture into the bowl with the sugar and whisk well. Whisk in the eggs.

5. In another bowl, whisk together the flour, baking powder, baking soda, and salt. Gently whisk the dry ingredients into the wet ones. Switch to a spatula and fold in the oil a little at a time. Fold in the orange segments and any juice left in the bowl. Scrape the batter into the pan and smooth the top.

6. Bake the cake for about 55 minutes, or until it is golden and a knife inserted into the center comes out clean. Cool on a wire rack for 5 minutes, then unmold onto the rack and cool to room temperature, right-side up. Serve with whipped cream and Honey–Blood Orange Compote, if desired.

note: To make Honey–Blood Orange Compote, suprême 3 more blood oranges according to the directions in step 3. Drizzle in 1 to 2 teaspoons honey. Let sit for 5 minutes, then stir gently.

Lemony olive oil banana bread with chocolate chips

If you don't have bananas so speckled with brown that you can barely see the yellow beneath, don't make this recipe. Hold off until you can smell the bananas in the fruit bowl from the moment you crack open the front door. When the whole house takes on that particular sweet, caramelized, vaguely decayed scent, you're ready to go.

Waiting for the bananas to turn ultra ripe before eating them all is about the hardest thing you'll need to do for this quick bread, especially if you're like me and love bananas. The recipe itself couldn't be more straightforward. The whole wheat adds a slightly warm, toasty flavor that works nicely with the sugary bananas. And the olive oil gives it a toehold on the savory side, while still calling the sweet side home. If you don't like lemons or don't like glazes, skip the glaze. Without it, the bread will be less cakelike and more classically banana bread–ish. Either way, it's the kind of thing you can throw together on a lazy Sunday afternoon.

Like most banana breads and nearly all sweet muffins, this is really cake in disguise. I'm calling it by its traditional designation so you'll know exactly what I'm talking about. But don't be fooled. Serve this for dessert or as a sweet afternoon nibble for teatime all week long.

serves 8 to 10

1 cup all-purpose flour

1 cup whole wheat flour

¾ cup packed dark brown sugar

¾ teaspoon baking soda

½ teaspoon kosher salt

1 cup coarsely chopped bittersweet chocolate

⅓ cup extra-virgin olive oil

2 large eggs, lightly beaten

1½ cups mashed, VERY ripe bananas (3 to 4 bananas)

¼ cup sour cream or plain full-fat yogurt

1 teaspoon freshly grated lemon zest

1 teaspoon vanilla extract

FOR THE GLAZE

1 cup confectioners' sugar

4 teaspoons freshly squeezed lemon juice

1. Preheat the oven to 350°F. Grease a 9 × 5-inch loaf pan.

(continued)

2. In a large bowl, whisk together the flours, brown sugar, baking soda, and salt. Add the chocolate pieces and combine well.

3. In a separate bowl, mix together the olive oil, eggs, mashed bananas, sour cream or yogurt, lemon zest, and vanilla. Pour the banana mixture into the flour mixture and fold with a spatula until just combined. Scrape the batter into the prepared pan and bake until dark golden brown and a tester inserted into the middle of the loaf comes out clean, 50 minutes to 1 hour.

4. Transfer the pan to a wire rack set over a rimmed baking sheet to cool for 10 minutes, then turn the loaf out of the pan onto the rack to cool completely, right-side up.

5. WHEN THE CAKE IS ALMOST COOL, MAKE THE GLAZE: In a bowl, whisk together the confectioners' sugar and lemon juice until smooth. Drizzle the glaze on top of the cake, spreading it with a spatula to cover.

Berry summer pudding with rose-scented custard

It wouldn't be the Fourth of July without a barbecue at my friends Karen and Dave's house, a convivial event that includes an icy bowl of strong punch, a spirited reading of the Declaration of Independence, copious amounts of grilled leg of lamb, and, for dessert, Karen's opulently purple berry summer pudding, dripping with crème anglaise.

This version is pretty faithful to Karen's recipe, with two tiny tweaks: I use soft whole wheat bread in place of white bread for the pudding mold and rose water in place of lavender flowers for the creamy sauce. Since the bread is covered with all those luscious berries, you can't really tell the difference between soft whole wheat and plain white, so I figured I might as well add a few grams of fiber. And since I didn't have any lavender flowers around when I made this, I reached for the most floral substitute I could find.

Karen goes out of her way to use fresh currants in the berry mix. Besides adding great flavor, they also bleed lots of juice, which is what you want to help cover up all the pale bread. So do the same if you can find them.

It's an ideal summer dessert because you can make it ahead, it doesn't require turning on the oven, and it takes excellent advantage of all the berries of the season. And if those aren't reasons enough to make it, here is one more: It's absolutely fantastic.

serves 8

FOR THE PUDDING

1½ pounds mixed fresh berries (about 5 cups)

½ cup sugar, plus more to taste

1 teaspoon freshly squeezed lemon juice, plus more to taste

10 to 15 slices soft whole wheat Pullman loaf, crusts removed

FOR THE CRÈME ANGLAISE (MAKES ABOUT 2½ CUPS)

1 cup whole milk

1 cup heavy cream

6 large egg yolks

½ cup sugar

Pinch fine sea salt

2 teaspoons rose water or vanilla extract, or to taste

1. MAKE THE PUDDING: Combine the berries, sugar, and ⅓ cup water in a medium saucepan. Simmer over medium heat until the sugar has completely dissolved and the berries release their juices, about 5 minutes. Stir in the lemon juice. The sauce should be sweet, with a hint of tartness. Adjust with more sugar or lemon juice as needed.

2. Spoon an even layer of the berry syrup (not the berries themselves) over the bottom of an 8-inch loaf pan. Line the bottom and sides of the pan with a single layer of bread; cut the bread into pieces as necessary to fit. Spoon a third of the fruit on top of the bread, making sure the bread is completely coated; top with a layer of bread. Spoon another third of the fruit over the bread; top with another layer of bread. Spoon the remaining fruit over the bread. Let the mixture cool completely, then wrap the pan tightly with plastic wrap. Place a light weight (a thick and preferably trashy paperback novel is perfect) on top of the pudding. Refrigerate overnight.

3. MAKE THE CRÈME ANGLAISE: Fill a large bowl with ice water. Bring the milk and cream to barely a simmer in a heavy-bottomed saucepan (bubbles will just begin to form around the edges).

4. In a bowl slightly smaller than the ice-water bath, whisk together the yolks, sugar, and salt. Slowly whisk in the hot milk until fully incorporated. Return the mixture to the pot. Cook over medium-high heat, stirring constantly, until the sauce is thick enough to coat the back of a spoon (170°F). Strain the sauce through a fine-mesh sieve into a metal bowl. Stir in the rose water. If it needs a bit more, go ahead and add it, but please have a light touch or it might wind up tasting like soap. Place the bowl into the water bath and stir occasionally until completely cool.

5. Run a knife around the sides of the summer pudding, then turn it over onto a plate to unmold. Serve in slices, with the crème anglaise on the side.

Triple chocolate trifle with raspberries

With its layers of cake, sherry, custard, and whipped cream, trifle is more than just pudding. It's a grand dessert, a celebration unto itself in a cut-crystal bowl. A genuine crowd-pleaser, large quantities can be assembled days in advance, making it an ideal dessert for a holiday party.

I thought about all this when I was planning a little soiree. Because the menu included latkes that would have me chained to the stove frying for most of the night, I wanted dessert to be something I could plop on the table with no last-minute fussing, and festive and compelling enough to seduce my carb-filled guests, many of whom would be under twelve.

With the kids in mind, I decided that a typical boozy trifle might not be the best thing. But I worried that simply leaving out the sherry would spoil the dessert's balance and character. What if I substituted a moister cake that didn't need either a libation or hydration, like brownies? And what if that cake contained yet another crowd pleaser, like chocolate pudding?

Though not in the least traditional, a chocolate pudding–brownie trifle would happily fill the bill. I added tart, juicy raspberries and nuggets of bittersweet chocolate to rein in the sumptuous sweetness.

By the time I pulled my gorgeous creation out of the fridge, my guests were groaning with potato pancake overload. But the sight of a glass bowl filled with chocolate and billowing whipped cream revived them all, kids and adults alike.

serves 8 to 10

FOR THE BROWNIES

1 cup (2 sticks) plus 2 tablespoons unsalted butter

3 ounces unsweetened chocolate, finely chopped

½ cup unsweetened cocoa powder, sifted

2½ cups granulated sugar

3 large eggs, beaten

1 tablespoon vanilla extract

1½ cups all-purpose flour

½ teaspoon kosher salt

3 tablespoons Cognac, rum, or bourbon (optional)

(continued)

FOR ASSEMBLY

½ cup granulated sugar

8 tablespoons (½ cup) unsweetened cocoa powder, sifted

2 tablespoons cornstarch

Pinch fine sea salt

1¾ cups whole milk

3 cups heavy cream

2 large egg yolks

10 ounces bittersweet chocolate, finely chopped (2 cups)

2 tablespoons unsalted butter

1 teaspoon vanilla extract

¼ cup confectioners' sugar

1 to 2 pints fresh raspberries

1. MAKE THE BROWNIES: Preheat the oven to 350°F. Grease a 9 × 13-inch baking pan.

2. In a large saucepan over medium heat, melt the butter. Remove the pan from the heat and stir in the chopped chocolate until fully melted. Stir in the cocoa powder and granulated sugar until combined. Slowly add the eggs, whisking the chocolate mixture constantly, then whisk in the vanilla. Fold in the flour and salt.

3. Pour the batter into the prepared pan. Bake until just firm, about 25 minutes (do not overbake). Transfer the pan to a wire rack to cool. If using the spirit, use a fork to prick holes in the hot brownies and drizzle the alcohol evenly over the pan.

4. ASSEMBLE THE TRIFLE: In a large bowl, mix together the granulated sugar, 3 tablespoons of the cocoa powder, the cornstarch, and the salt. Whisk in ¾ cup of the milk. In a large saucepan, bring the remaining 1 cup milk and ½ cup of the cream to a boil over medium heat. Whisk the hot milk mixture slowly into the cocoa mixture. Return to the saucepan. Cook over medium heat, whisking gently, until slightly thickened, about 2 minutes (you may see a simmering bubble or two; that's okay, but don't let it boil).

5. In a heatproof medium bowl, whisk the yolks. Whisking them constantly, very slowly dribble about half the chocolate mixture into the yolks until fully combined. Pour the yolk mixture into the saucepan, whisking constantly. Cook over medium-low heat, whisking occasionally, until thickened, about 5 minutes. (Do not let the mixture come to a simmer at this point. If the pan begins to steam thickly, remove from the heat for a few moments and stir well before continuing.) Transfer to a bowl and let cool slightly.

6. Melt 5 ounces (1 cup) of the chopped chocolate with the butter. Stir until smooth. Stir in the vanilla. Cool for 5 minutes, then fold the mixture into the thickened egg mixture. Place plastic wrap directly against the pudding (to keep a skin from forming) and chill until set, about 3 hours. (The pudding and brownies can be made up to 2 days ahead.)

(continued)

7. Just before assembling, in the bowl of an electric mixer fitted with the whisk attachment, beat the remaining 2½ cups cream with the remaining 5 tablespoons cocoa powder and the confectioners' sugar until the cream holds soft peaks. Scrape down the sides and fold in any excess cocoa or sugar.

8. Cut the brownies into 1-inch squares. Fit a layer of brownie squares in the bottom of a 4-quart trifle dish, glass, or other bowl. Top with half the pudding, a third of the cream, a third of the remaining chopped chocolate, and a third of the raspberries. Repeat the layering until all the ingredients have been used, ending with a layer of brownies, whipped cream, chocolate, and raspberries. Serve immediately, or cover with plastic wrap and chill for up to 24 hours before serving.

Brown butter maple roasted pears

This is yet another variation on a honey-roasted pear recipe I stole—I mean, adapted—from the genius pastry chef Claudia Fleming of The North Fork Table and Inn. Years ago, when Claudia was the pastry chef at Gramercy Tavern and I was a newly minted freelancer for the *New York Times*, I helped her write her cookbook *The Last Course*. I think it's a wonderful book, and not just because I had a hand in writing it. It's because Claudia is brilliant at both technique and combining flavors, and that shines through in every recipe.

In Claudia's original roasted pear dish, she cooks the pears in rich, dark, chestnut honey, then finishes them with butter and fresh thyme. In my version I swap out the musky honey for smoky Grade B maple syrup—Grade B is best for cooking and baking, as it's darker and more richly flavored than Grade A. I also brown the butter, which adds an autumnal, nutty complexity.

You can serve these with whipped cream on top of pound cake, or with little crisp cookies on the side. (The Pistachio Shortbread on page 202 would be ideal.) All those things would be delightful. But all the pears really need for maximum enjoyment is a spoon. A bowl wouldn't hurt, either.

serves 6

3 almost-ripe Bosc or Anjou pears, or a mixture of the two (1½ pounds)

4 tablespoons (½ stick) unsalted butter

⅔ cup pure maple syrup

1 cinnamon stick

⅛ teaspoon kosher salt

¾ teaspoon freshly squeezed lemon juice

1. Preheat the oven to 375°F.

2. Peel the pears and halve them lengthwise. Use a melon baller or spoon to scoop out the core.

3. In a large skillet over medium-high heat, melt 3 tablespoons of the butter. Cook until frothy. Reduce the heat to medium and cook until the milk solids sink to the bottom of the pan and turn a nutty brown, 5 to 7 minutes. Brown butter can burn quickly, so watch it carefully. Add the pears, cut-side down, to the pan. Cook, without moving, until the undersides are golden, about 3 minutes. Flip the pears and cook, without moving, for 3 minutes more.

(continued)

4. Pour the maple syrup over the pan and drop in the cinnamon stick. Flip the pears again and transfer the skillet to the oven. Bake until the pears are just tender, 10 to 12 minutes.

5. Use a slotted spoon to transfer the pears to a plate. Return the skillet to the heat. Add the salt. Simmer over medium-high heat until the sauce is syrupy, 3 to 5 minutes. Whisk in the remaining 1 tablespoon butter and the lemon juice. Spoon the sauce over the pears and serve.

Obsessive twice-baked sour cherry pie

Truth be told, I was only 90 percent happy with the sour cherry pie recipe I published in my "Good Appetite" column in the *New York Times*. The crust, a twice-baked beauty using a technique I learned from White House pastry chef Bill Yosses, was terrific—crisp, buttery, able to stand up to all those sweet cherry juices. And the filling, made with Minute tapioca (aka instant tapioca), was shining, clear, and just firm enough. But the filling texture still had tiny little tapioca beads floating in it, like a cherry-flavored tapioca pudding. You'd barely notice them if you weren't looking. But I was looking. During the blink-your-eyes-and-you'll-miss-it sour cherry season, I want my once-a-year sour cherry pie to be perfect.

Thus began my obsessive experimentation for a clear, tasteless, and perfectly smooth cherry pie filling. So I tried a lot of thickeners: flour, cornstarch, potato starch, and tapioca starch (aka tapioca flour). I was gravely disappointed in all.

One thing I found interesting was that tapioca starch was not just ground-up instant tapioca pearls. Tapioca pearls, the kind used to make pudding, are treated to become more stable. So I decided to grind up 2 tablespoons instant tapioca in a clean coffee grinder until it turned to powder. Then I mixed the powder into the cherries.

The result? A clear, glossy, and thickened filling. To finish it off, I added a bit of lard in the crust to make it extra flaky.

In a word: *Yum*. Or possibly: *Insane*. Either shoe is a likely fit.

serves 8

FOR THE PIECRUST

1¾ cups plus 2 tablespoons all-purpose flour, plus more for dusting

⅜ teaspoon kosher salt

13 tablespoons unsalted butter, chilled and cut into pieces

2 tablespoons lard, chilled (or use more butter)

3 to 6 tablespoons ice water, as needed

FOR THE FILLING

2 to 3 tablespoons instant tapioca (more if you like it very set, less if you don't mind a little thickened juice)

1 cup granulated sugar (or more if you like a sweeter pie)

¼ teaspoon ground cinnamon

2 pounds sour cherries (about 6 cups), rinsed and pitted

1 tablespoon kirsch or brandy

3 tablespoons heavy cream

Demerara or raw sugar, for sprinkling

(continued)

1. MAKE THE DOUGH FOR THE PIECRUST: In a food processor, pulse together the flour and salt just to combine. Add the butter and lard and pulse until lima bean–size pieces form. Add the water 1 tablespoon at a time, pulsing until the mixture just comes together. Pat the dough into 2 discs, one using two-thirds of the dough, the other using one-third of the dough (weigh it if you have a kitchen scale; one disc should be about 12 ounces, the other 6 ounces). Wrap the discs in plastic and refrigerate for at least 1 hour and up to 3 days before rolling out and baking.

2. Preheat the oven to 425°F.

3. Place the larger dough disc on a lightly floured surface and roll it into a 12-inch circle about ⅜ inch thick. Transfer the dough to a 9-inch pie plate. Line the dough with foil and weigh it down with pie weights (I use pennies, but dry beans or rice will also work). Bake until the crust is light golden brown, about 30 minutes.

4. WHILE THE PIECRUST IS BAKING, MAKE THE FILLING: Using a clean coffee or spice grinder, grind the tapioca to a fine powder. In a small bowl, combine the tapioca with the granulated sugar and cinnamon. Place the cherries in a bowl and add the sugar-tapioca mixture. Drizzle in the kirsch or brandy and toss gently to combine.

5. When the piecrust is ready, transfer it to a wire rack to cool slightly and reduce the oven temperature to 375°F. Remove the foil and pie weights and scrape the cherry filling into the piecrust.

6. Place the smaller disc of dough on a lightly floured surface and roll it out to ⅜ inch thick. Use a round cookie cutter (or several round cookie cutters of different sizes) to cut out circles of dough. Arrange the dough circles on top of the cherry filling.

7. Brush the dough circles with cream and sprinkle the top of the pie generously with Demerara sugar. Bake until the crust is dark golden brown and the filling begins to bubble, 50 minutes to 1 hour. Transfer the pie to a wire rack to cool for at least 2 hours to allow the filling to set up before serving.

Spiced maple pecan pie with star anise

I never thought to simmer down maple syrup until it turns thick, viscous, and extremely maple-y until I made Bill Yosses's maple ice cream recipe. Yosses, a former White House pastry chef and a good friend of mine (we wrote a cookbook together), reduces the syrup to eliminate as much of its water content as possible, which gives the smoothest, silkiest-textured ice cream imaginable, with an intense maple flavor. He also recommends reducing maple syrup for any recipe in which you want an extremely vibrant maple character.

After trying his amazing ice cream recipe, I began to think about what else might benefit from reduced maple syrup's profound caramel sweetness, and came up with pecan pie.

The problem with most maple pecan pies is that the maple becomes shy and quiet in the company of all those assertive toasted nuts. Simmering down the syrup, I hoped, would help it hold its own. So I tried it, and it worked beautifully.

Then one Thanksgiving, I decided to add a layer of complexity by infusing whole spices into the maple syrup while it was simmering. I thought the sharp, woodsy fennel flavor of star anise would add an unexpected nuance.

That's just what happened. My pie was warm and licorice-y from the anise, toasty from the roasted pecans, and as syrupy, sugary, and toothachingly sweet as a proper pecan pie should be. I wouldn't have it any other way, though a dollop of crème fraîche tempers the gooey filling without compromising its integrity.

serves 8

FOR THE PIECRUST

1¼ cups all-purpose flour, plus more for dusting

¼ teaspoon fine sea salt

10 tablespoons (1¼ sticks) cold unsalted butter, cut into ½-inch pieces

2 to 5 tablespoons ice water

FOR THE FILLING

1 cup pure maple syrup

½ cup Demerara or raw sugar

8 whole star anise

2 cups pecan halves

3 large eggs

4 tablespoons (½ stick) unsalted butter, melted

2 tablespoons dark aged rum

¼ teaspoon kosher salt

Whipped crème fraîche, for serving

1. MAKE THE PIECRUST: In a food processor, briefly pulse together the flour and salt. Add the butter and pulse until the mixture forms lima bean–size pieces (three to five 1-second pulses). Add the ice water 1 tablespoon at a time, pulsing until the mixture is just moist enough to hold together. Form the dough into a ball, wrap with plastic, and flatten into a disc. Refrigerate for at least 1 hour (or up to a week, or freeze it for up to 4 months) before rolling out and baking.

2. On a lightly floured surface, roll out the dough to a 12-inch circle. Transfer the crust to a 9-inch pie plate. Fold over any excess dough, then crimp as decoratively as you can manage.

3. Prick the crust all over with a fork. Freeze the crust for 15 minutes or refrigerate for 30 minutes.

4. Preheat the oven to 400°F.

5. Cover the pie with foil and fill with pie weights (you can use pennies, rice, or dried beans for this; I use pennies). Bake for 20 minutes; remove the foil and weights and bake until pale golden, about 5 minutes more. Cool on a wire rack until needed. Reduce the oven temperature to 325°F.

6. MAKE THE FILLING: In a medium saucepan over medium-high heat, bring the maple syrup, Demerara sugar, and star anise to a boil. Reduce the heat to maintain a simmer and cook until the mixture is very thick, all the sugar has dissolved, and the mixture reduces to 1 cup, 15 to 20 minutes. Remove from the heat and let sit for 1 hour for the anise to infuse.

7. While the syrup is infusing, spread the pecans on a rimmed baking sheet and toast them in the oven until they start to smell nutty, about 12 minutes. Transfer to a wire rack to cool. Keep the oven on.

8. Remove the star anise from the syrup. Warm the syrup if necessary to make it pourable but not hot (you can pop it in the microwave for a few seconds if you've moved it to a measuring cup). In a medium bowl, whisk together the syrup, eggs, melted butter, rum, and salt. Fold in the pecan halves. Pour the filling into the crust and transfer to a rimmed baking sheet. Bake until the pie is firm to the touch but jiggles slightly when moved, 35 to 40 minutes. Let cool to room temperature before serving with whipped crème fraîche.

Pistachio shortbread

If I had a signature dish, it would be shortbread. Buttery, rich, crumbly shortbread is not only pretty much my favorite thing on earth to eat, it's also about the easiest thing a pastry cook can make. And I've made it in every possible variation I can think of, and as new ideas pop into my head, I will practically run to the kitchen to bake up those, too. Right now I've got a coconut curry shortbread idea floating around up there.

This shortbread recipe is one of my all-time favorites, a classic and gorgeous combination of pistachio nuts and orange blossom water. But remove the pistachios and orange blossom water, and the recipe can be a blank canvas for all kinds of variations. Flavor it with vanilla, rose water, or any aged spirit, or swap in another type of nut. Spices are marvelous—grated nutmeg, cinnamon, ginger, mace, cardamom, alone or in combination—as are citrus zest and a splash of juice.

But this particular combination reminds me of Morocco, where I've never been but dream about in sweet, perfumed reveries. This shortbread is as close as I've come, but until the day I take the trip, it's not a bad recompense.

makes 1 (8-inch) pan

2 cups all-purpose flour

¾ cup confectioners' sugar

½ cup shelled, raw pistachios

¾ teaspoon kosher salt

1 cup (2 sticks) cold unsalted butter, cut into ½-inch cubes

2 teaspoons orange blossom water

1. Preheat the oven to 325°F.

2. In a food processor, combine the flour, confectioners' sugar, pistachios, and salt. Pulse until the nuts are coarsely to finely chopped. Pulse in the butter and orange blossom water until a moist ball forms.

3. Press the dough evenly into an 8-inch-square baking pan. Prick the shortbread all over with a fork. Bake until barely golden, 45 to 50 minutes. Slice the shortbread while warm.

Lemon curd squares with rosemary

Lucy's lemon squares from the *Peanuts Cook Book* was far and away my mother's favorite cookie to make when my sister and I were kids. She'd whip up a batch for birthday parties and bake sales, whenever a homemade sweet was called for, and everyone in the family loved them—even Mocha, our old chocolate Labrador. Once he polished off an entire batch that my mother had stashed out of sight to bring to some event or other. When she saw the empty plate, she scolded my sister and me—then discovered the guilty pup licking his confectioners' sugar–dusted nose. I might still be holding a grudge.

This has not, however, diminished my fondness for lemon squares, which I've made every which way since I was old enough to bake.

This recipe is the culmination of all my trials. It's based on Lucy's in citrusy spirit, though I've monkeyed with the technique and ingredients. Instead of a thin, brittle crust with a lemonade-sweet filling, I've made a thick and buttery shortbread laced with piney fresh rosemary, topped with a bracing lemon curd that's just sweet enough.

It's definitely more sophisticated than either my mother or Lucy would have made back in the day. But I'm sure Mocha would have liked it just as well.

makes 24 squares

FOR THE SHORTBREAD

3 cups all-purpose flour

1½ cups (3 sticks) unsalted butter

½ cup granulated sugar

⅓ cup confectioners' sugar, plus more for sprinkling

1 tablespoon chopped fresh rosemary

1 teaspoon finely grated lemon zest

FOR THE LEMON CURD

6 large eggs, lightly beaten

1½ cups granulated sugar

1 tablespoon finely grated lemon zest

⅔ cup freshly squeezed lemon juice (from 3 or 4 lemons)

¼ cup all-purpose flour

Pinch kosher salt

1. Preheat the oven to 325°F and lightly grease a 9 × 13-inch baking pan.

2. MAKE THE SHORTBREAD: In a food processor, combine the flour, butter, granulated sugar, confectioners' sugar, rosemary, and lemon zest. Pulse until a crumbly dough forms. Press the dough into the prepared pan and bake until the shortbread is golden around the edges, about 40 minutes.

3. WHILE THE SHORTBREAD IS BAKING, MAKE THE LEMON CURD: In a large bowl, whisk together the eggs, granulated sugar, lemon zest and juice, flour, and salt.

4. When the shortbread is ready, take it out of the oven and increase the oven temperature to 350°F. Carefully pour the lemon curd onto the shortbread base and return the pan to the oven. Bake until the topping is just set, about 20 minutes. Allow to cool to room temperature before cutting into squares. Cover and refrigerate the bars for up to 3 days. Sprinkle with confectioners' sugar before serving.

Coconut fudge brownies

Dense and chewy, these brownies are closer to chocolate truffles or a bowl of ganache frosting than they are to crumbly little cakes. The coconut oil gives them more chew than even the moistest usual recipe and a flavor that's as tasty as a Mounds bar. The sweetened shredded coconut—don't under any circumstances try to substitute dry unsweetened desiccated coconut from the health food store—gives them a melt-in-the-mouth texture.

They don't cut as neatly as cakey brownies but their intense fudge flavor more than makes up for their messy appearance (or at least I think so).

Whatever you do, don't overbake these. You want them just on the solid side of chocolate sauce. Overbaking destroys their charms. As my friend Robin said when she accidentally overbaked a batch, "They taste like Passover brownies." Which is not a good thing. And if you do underbake them slightly and they run when you cut them, pretend you meant them to be like that all along (and serve them with a spoon).

"Do you like my molten chocolate brownies?" you can ask your friends. I promise you, they will.

makes about 24 brownies

⅓ cup unsweetened cocoa powder

½ cup plus 2 tablespoons boiling water

2 ounces unsweetened chocolate, finely chopped

4 tablespoons (½ stick) unsalted butter, melted

½ cup plus 2 tablespoons coconut oil

2 large eggs

2 large egg yolks

2 teaspoons vanilla extract

2½ cups sugar

1¾ cups all-purpose flour

¾ teaspoon kosher salt

3 ounces bittersweet chocolate, cut into ½-inch pieces

2 cups sweetened shredded coconut

Fleur de sel, for sprinkling

1. Preheat the oven to 350°F. Lightly grease a 9 × 13-inch baking pan.

2. In a large bowl, whisk together the cocoa powder and boiling water until smooth. Add the unsweetened chocolate and whisk until the chocolate has melted. Whisk in the melted butter and coconut oil. (The mixture may look curdled.) Add the eggs, egg yolks, and vanilla and continue to whisk until combined. Whisk in the sugar until fully incorporated. Add the flour and salt and fold with a spatula until just combined. Fold in the bittersweet chocolate pieces.

3. Scrape half the batter into the prepared pan and smooth it into an even layer with a spatula. Sprinkle 1 cup of the shredded coconut on top of the batter. Spread the remaining batter over the coconut. Top with the remaining 1 cup shredded coconut. Sprinkle with fleur de sel and bake until a tester inserted into the center of the brownie is just set and shiny, 30 to 35 minutes. If you test it with a toothpick, it will seem wet, but that's okay. It solidifies as it cools. Transfer the pan to a wire rack to cool completely before cutting into squares.

Mallobars

This is my version of homemade Mallomars. But instead of painstakingly forming individual cookies, I use the bar cookie method, spreading everything in one large pan. I end up with a crisp, homemade graham cracker crust topped by honey marshmallow and a thick layer of chocolate. Though they are easier than the original recipe, I wouldn't call them a super-quick dessert. You still need to devote a good part of an afternoon to their confection. Or try to make the components over several days if it's easier to carve that out of your schedule.

However you manage it, the payoff is big: They are truly scrumptious, and I guarantee that if you bring them to a potluck or party, no one else will have brought anything remotely like them. They are unusual, crowd-pleasing, fancy looking, and even slightly good for you (okay, just slightly) from the whole wheat flour.

makes about 18 (2-inch) squares

FOR THE GRAHAM CRACKER BASE

1 cup (2 sticks) unsalted butter

¼ cup firmly packed dark brown sugar

¼ cup granulated sugar

¼ cup honey

1½ cups whole wheat flour, plus more for dusting

1 cup all-purpose flour

1 teaspoon kosher salt

½ teaspoon ground cinnamon

FOR THE HONEY MARSHMALLOW

3 envelopes unflavored gelatin (about 3 tablespoons)

1 cup cold water

2 cups granulated sugar

¼ cup honey

2 large egg whites

¼ teaspoon kosher salt

1 tablespoon vanilla extract

FOR THE CHOCOLATE GLAZE

9 ounces bittersweet chocolate, chopped

¾ cup heavy cream

1. MAKE THE GRAHAM CRACKER BASE: In the bowl of an electric mixer fitted with the paddle attachment, cream the butter, sugars, and honey until smooth. In a medium bowl, combine the flours, salt, and cinnamon. Add the dry ingredients to the mixer bowl and beat until the dough just comes together.

2. Wrap the dough in plastic and pat it into a disc. Chill the dough for at least 1 hour and up to 2 days.

3. When ready to bake, preheat the oven to 325°F. Line a 9 × 13-inch baking pan with foil or parchment paper.

4. On a lightly floured surface, or between two sheets of parchment paper, roll out the dough into a rectangle that just fits the prepared pan. Carefully transfer the dough to the prepared pan. Squish it to fit if it starts to tear (the dough is soft). Prick the dough all over with a fork. Bake the graham cracker base until golden brown, 18 to 20 minutes. Allow the crust to cool completely before topping with the marshmallow. (The graham cracker base can be made a few days ahead; store, covered in foil, at room temperature.)

5. WHILE THE GRAHAM CRACKER BASE COOLS, MAKE THE HONEY MARSHMALLOW: Place the gelatin in the cold water to bloom. In a saucepan over medium heat, combine the granulated sugar, honey, and ½ cup water. Clip a candy thermometer to the side and cook, stirring to dissolve the sugar, until the mixture reaches 240°F.

6. In the bowl of an electric mixer fitted with the whisk attachment, whisk the egg whites and salt until they hold soft peaks. When the sugar mixture has come up to temperature, with the mixer running, carefully pour it into the egg whites. Continue whisking until the mixture has cooled slightly, about 1 minute, then add the gelatin mixture and the vanilla. Continue whisking until the mixture begins to thicken and quadruples in volume, 5 to 7 minutes. Scrape the marshmallow onto the graham cracker base and smooth the top with a spatula. Allow the marshmallow to set for 4 hours or up to overnight, covered, at room temperature.

7. MEANWHILE, MAKE THE CHOCOLATE GLAZE: Place the chocolate pieces in a bowl. In a saucepan over medium-high heat, bring the cream just to a boil. Pour the cream over the chocolate and whisk until the chocolate has melted and the glaze is smooth and shiny. Pour the glaze over the set marshmallow and smooth with a spatula. Allow the glaze to set, about 30 minutes, before cutting into squares.

Whole wheat peanut butter sandies

Of all the birthday presents Dahlia got when she turned two—the books and stuffed animals, the adorable BPA-free tea set—the gift that I enjoyed the most was a little paper bag filled with crumbly, brittle, lightly salted peanut butter cookies from her friend Alice's mama, Anna.

To be honest, after all the cupcakes, ice cream, and tortilla chips Dahlia ate at her party, I didn't actually share those cookies with her at all, but tucked them away in the back of a kitchen drawer to be savored by us grown-ups after bedtime disposed of the child.

Not that there was anything unwholesome about them. Anna, who was, incidentally, the pastry chef at Al Di La in Brooklyn (one of my favorite Italian restaurants in the city), made them with whole wheat flour, natural peanut butter, raw sugar, and eggs, and they were about as good for you as a cookie can be. I just wanted to give Dahlia a few days to recover from her party before feeding her any more sugar. By that time, they were gone.

I felt very guilty about eating her present, so I set about righting the wrong by making another batch. Anna nicely gave me the recipe and I made them as soon as I could. And Dahlia adored them—not that she had anything to compare them to.

makes about 42 cookies

1¼ cups whole wheat pastry flour	½ cup natural salted peanut butter
1 teaspoon baking soda	1 cup Demerara or raw sugar
¼ teaspoon plus a pinch kosher salt	1 large egg
½ cup (1 stick) unsalted butter, at room temperature	1 teaspoon vanilla extract

1. In a large bowl, sift together the flour, baking soda, and salt.

2. In the bowl of an electric mixer fitted with the paddle attachment, cream the butter. Beat in the peanut butter until smooth. Add the Demerara sugar and beat well. Beat in the egg and vanilla until fully incorporated. Stop and scrape down the bowl. Slowly beat in the dry ingredients.

3. Transfer the dough to a large sheet of plastic wrap or waxed paper. Shape the dough into a 12-inch-long log. Wrap the dough in the plastic, using the wrap to help form the most uniform-size log possible. Transfer the dough to the refrigerator and chill at least 2 hours.

4. When you are ready to bake the cookies, preheat the oven to 350°F.

5. Slice the dough into ¼-inch-thick rounds and transfer them to an ungreased baking sheet, spacing them 1 inch apart. Bake the cookies until lightly colored and semifirm, about 15 minutes; rotate the sheets halfway through baking. Transfer the cookies to a wire rack to cool completely.

cocktails
AND snacks

Rye Manhattan

Ask any hipster bartender worth his arm garters what's the best booze to mix into a Manhattan, and the answer will be rye. Although bourbon has usurped rye as today's Manhattan foundation, rye has history. According to David Wondrich, the erudite cocktail historian (and my friend and neighbor), when the Manhattan cocktail was created in 1874, it was made with rye whiskey, the most popular spirit of the era. This was a good thing. Bourbon Manhattans, opines Dave, are so sickly sweet that no amount of fiddling with the bitters and vermouth can save them. Luckily, there are a number of excellent rye whiskies on the market, and if you can find a high-proof rye, Dave recommends that above all (don't plan on operating any heavy machinery after your tipple).

This is my husband, Daniel's, adaptation of Dave's Manhattan, jiggered to meet our exact tastes. Daniel makes a lot of these, especially in winter when cocktails infused with brown spirits warm the soul better than white spirits (or so we think). Garnished with a homemade maraschino cherry, it redeems even the most frustrating, exhausting, harried day.

serves 1

2 ounces rye whiskey, plus a dash

Scant 1 ounce sweet vermouth

2 dashes Angostura bitters

1 maraschino cherry, preferably homemade

Stir the rye, vermouth, and bitters well with plenty of cracked ice. Strain into a chilled cocktail glass and garnish with a cherry.

Kumquat-clementine cordial

In a blissful and more organized alternate reality that I do not inhabit, I would have thought about a homemade libation for the holidays in August. That's when, surrounded by ripe, seasonal fruit, and with plenty of maceration time, I could have created a delightful elixir to distribute to my nearest and dearest in December and bring joy their world.

Luckily, in Mireille Johnston's classic cookbook *The Cuisine of the Sun*, she suggests many easy libation recipes, some with winter-friendly citrus fruit, like one where oranges are steeped in brandy with coriander seeds. The headnote advised drinking this whenever one "feels melancholy, anxious, or even merry—truly wonderful for all occasions."

But the maceration time was a biblical forty days. I needed to whip it up in an hour and have it ready in a week. Citrus juice, good-quality booze, and sugar couldn't taste bad, even immediately, I reassured myself.

I settled on pretty kumquats and juicy clementines for my rum cordial, and added star anise, cinnamon, coriander, and allspice berries for dimension. Then I capped the bottles and left them on the counter, giving them a good shake every day to encourage the infusing.

A week later, the flavors had metamorphosed into something deeply perfumed and rich with spice and citrus. Although they deviated from Mireille Johnston's original recipe, my cordials still fit her description to a T—truly wonderful for all occasions.

serves 12

¼ cup sugar, preferably superfine

1 tablespoon boiling water

3 tablespoons freshly squeezed clementine juice (from 1 to 2 clementines)

6 kumquats, thinly sliced and seeded

1 clementine, thinly sliced

1¾ cups white rum (375 ml)

3 whole allspice berries

2 whole star anise, broken in half if necessary to fit through the bottle neck

1. Have ready a glass bottle with a cork or jar with a lid for macerating. Place the sugar in a large glass measuring cup or bowl. Stir in the boiling water for 1 minute. Add the clementine juice and continue stirring until the sugar dissolves, about 1 minute more.

2. If using a bottle for storage, shove the kumquat and clementine slices through the top (you might have to curl them into cylinders first). Add the sugar syrup and remaining ingredients. Cover and shake once a day for a week before serving.

3. Serve as is, over ice, with a splash of seltzer, topped with chilled white wine or sparkling wine, or topped with boiling water as a hot toddy.

Speedy coconut eggnog

There is nothing I don't like about eggnog. It's rich, it's creamy, it's fluffy and frothy. It is, for me, the pinnacle of wintertime tippling. But for my dairy-eschewing husband? Not so much.

One winter, right when the weather started to turn snowy, I was experimenting with a butterscotch-Scotch eggnog recipe for my column in the *New York Times* when I felt a little sorry for Daniel, who was sipping a decidedly unexciting bourbon on the rocks. So I concocted this dairy-free nog for him using unsweetened coconut milk, which is my favorite dairy replacer.

It tastes like a version of a *coquito* (a Puerto Rican nog that uses Coco Lopez), only much less sweet. And it's nearly as fluffy, frothy, and festive as a traditional nog—only even better, because this one we can share.

serves 2, but can be scaled up or down

2 large eggs

¾ cup unsweetened coconut milk

1 tablespoon sugar, or to taste

1 shot rum or bourbon

1 shot brandy

Freshly grated nutmeg, for garnish

Place the eggs, coconut milk, sugar, rum or bourbon, and brandy in a blender and puree until smooth. Serve garnished with lots of nutmeg and with an ice cube, if you like your nog a little chilly.

Sweet-and-spicy candied nuts

These fragrant, glossy candied nuts make the perfect holiday gift when scooped into a pretty glass jar and tied with a silky, bright ribbon. In addition to snacking, they are delicious in a salad of bitter greens with a nice tart vinaigrette, or layered with sliced fruit and yogurt for a breakfast parfait. I have sprinkled them over roasted root vegetables and even chopped them up to garnish cakes. You can't go wrong.

I made a batch one December, intending to pack them up for friends. But the batch was small, and by the time I'd "tasted" enough of them to make sure they were worthy, there were hardly any left. Instead, I put the remainders in a glass bowl on the table next to the Christmas Eve eggnog and let everyone snack on them while imbibing. The crunchy, candied nuts were a huge hit, gone in minutes with people asking for more. Alas, there weren't any.

But next year, I'm going to make a double batch and give them out to everyone I know. Or perhaps I should make that a triple.

makes 5 cups

1 cup packed light brown sugar	½ teaspoon ground cinnamon
1 large egg white	½ teaspoon freshly grated nutmeg
1 pound mixed nuts	Large pinch cayenne
1 teaspoon kosher salt	Pinch ground cloves

1. Preheat the oven to 300°F. Line a baking sheet with parchment paper.

2. In a large bowl, whisk together the brown sugar and egg white. Add the nuts and toss to combine. In a separate bowl, stir together the salt, cinnamon, nutmeg, cayenne, and cloves. Sprinkle the mixture over the nuts and toss well.

3. Spread the nuts in a single layer on the prepared baking sheet. Bake, tossing occasionally, until the nuts are fragrant and almost dry to the touch, about 30 minutes.

Healthy homemade Cheddar crisps

Once I realized how easy it was to make my own crackers (even easier than certain finicky chocolate chip cookie recipes I know and love), I decided to branch out from the oat biscuits I had been serving with cheese. My goal was to make a self-sufficient cracker snack that had the cheese already mixed into it, something suitable for adult- and kid-munching alike.

I based my recipe on cheese pennies—those savory, cheese-filled shortbread-like crackers with a thick crumbly texture.

Usually, I like cheese pennies only when they are hot. For some unknown quirk of physics, once they cool, their flavor mysteriously disappears. To compensate, I increased the amount of cheese stirred into the dough, and then topped the crackers with even more cheese while they were baking. The cheese topping turned golden brown and crunchy, adding a salty, tangy kick that stayed with the cracker at any temperature (an asset on the playground and buffet table both).

I also substituted whole wheat flour for the white flour, hence the recipe title. At least, they are more healthful (and tastier, says I) than Goldfish.

If you have more time, try rolling out the dough to ⅛ inch thick, stamping shapes using small cookie cutters, and baking as directed. The children in your life will appreciate these cuter variations—and the adults might, too.

makes about 48 crackers

1 cup whole wheat flour	½ teaspoon kosher salt
¼ teaspoon baking powder	Pinch cayenne (optional)
4 tablespoons (½ stick) unsalted butter, at room temperature	1½ cups shredded Cheddar cheese (6 ounces)

1. In a small bowl, combine the flour and baking powder. In a food processor or the bowl of an electric mixer fitted with the paddle attachment, mix the butter, salt, and cayenne until creamy. Add 1 cup of the cheese and mix until thoroughly combined. Gradually add the flour mixture and run the food processor or beat with the paddle until the dough pulls away from the sides of the bowl and starts to form a ball, about 7 minutes. Wrap the dough in plastic and roll into a log about 1½ inches in diameter. Refrigerate for 1 hour or up to overnight.

2. Preheat the oven to 350°F. Line two baking sheets with parchment paper.

3. Unwrap the log of dough and slice it into rounds ³⁄₁₆ inch thick. Arrange the rounds on the prepared baking sheets and place a generous pinch of the remaining ½ cup cheese on each cracker. Bake until the crackers are golden brown, about 12 minutes. Turn off the oven and leave the crackers to crisp for 5 minutes more. Transfer the crackers to a wire rack to cool.

Pan-roasted radish and anchovy crostini

The first time I ate a roasted radish at a friend's house for dinner, I thought it was a baby turnip—a sweet, tender, caramelized turnip with a faint mustard edge to give it verve.

I gobbled up an entire plateful before realizing that, in fact, I was eating radishes. The pink skins and oblong shape finally clued me in.

It's probably a good thing I didn't know what I was nibbling before I was hooked. Because before I discovered otherwise, cooked radishes did not sound at all appealing. In my mind, radishes were supposed to be crunchy, taut, and a little bitter, a cleansing vegetable to cut the fat of rich foods. These sweet little orbs were none of those things. But they were completely beguiling in their own right.

Now, come June, when radishes are available at the farmers' market in ruby profusion, cooking them has become an integral part of my radish repertoire. Usually I pan-roast them, which is faster than oven roasting and adds more color, too. They are so flavorful on their own that they don't need more than a slick of olive oil and a sprinkle of salt to bring them to life.

But if you are one for flavorful excess, and I most certainly am, layering them onto crisp crostini and adding a pungent, buttery anchovy sauce will probably make you smile—in between bites, that is.

serves 4 to 6

1 bunch radishes

¼ cup plus 1½ tablespoons extra-virgin olive oil

½ teaspoon kosher salt

¼ teaspoon freshly ground black pepper

4 tablespoons (½ stick) unsalted butter

8 anchovy fillets, finely chopped

4 fat garlic cloves, finely chopped

Pinch crushed red pepper flakes

Freshly squeezed lemon juice, to taste

8 (½-inch-thick) slices crusty bread, toasted

4 teaspoons chopped fresh parsley

1. Remove the leaves and stems from the radishes; trim the tails. Cut larger radishes lengthwise into sixths and smaller radishes lengthwise into quarters.

2. Heat a large skillet over medium-high heat until very hot. Add 1½ tablespoons of the oil. Add the radishes in a single layer (do not crowd the skillet); season with the salt and black pepper. Cook the radishes, without moving, until lightly colored on the undersides, about 3 minutes. Shake the pan and continue cooking until fork-tender, about 3 minutes more.

3. In a small skillet or saucepan over medium heat, melt the butter. Stir in the remaining ¼ cup oil, the anchovies, garlic, and red pepper flakes. Reduce the heat to low and gently simmer until warm, about 4 minutes. Stir in lemon juice to taste.

4. Brush each slice of toast with the warm anchovy sauce and top with several radish wedges. Spoon additional sauce on top. Sprinkle each toast with parsley and serve.

Roasted pepper and celery leaf crostini

I adore roasted red peppers, but haven't made a proper batch in years. It's not that they are hard to do, just messy and time consuming. You have to blister the red peppers until the skins char black, then steam them in a bowl or bag until they cool, then slither off the ashen skins with your fingers, but not under running water or you will lose a lot of flavor. Inevitably, this peeling takes much longer than I think it will; plus, the tarry bits of skin stick everywhere—counters, dishtowels, under my fingernails. Cleanup is a pain.

But I love the rich, earthy flavor of roasted peppers, especially when they're piled high on garlic-rubbed crostini, maybe decorated with celery leaves and salty anchovies (or capers).

So for the last few red pepper seasons I've struck a compromise that suits my current, lazier cooking style much better. I roast the peppers until melting, caramelized, and jammy, but I don't peel them. They come out a little bit like a confit, with an intense red pepper taste. They are not as velvet textured and refined as proper roasted peppers, but they are so much easier that I find myself making them all the time (even on weeknights) and not just for a fancy party or special occasion. These days, easy satisfaction is where I'm at.

makes 6 crostini

2 medium red bell peppers, seeded and cut into ¼-inch-wide strips

4 teaspoons extra-virgin olive oil, plus more for drizzling

½ teaspoon kosher salt

½ teaspoon smoked sweet paprika

¼ cup chopped celery leaves

6 (¼-inch-thick) slices crusty bread

1 garlic clove, halved

Anchovy fillets or drained capers, for serving (optional)

1. Preheat the oven to 375°F.

2. In a bowl, toss the peppers with the olive oil, salt, and paprika. Spread on a large baking sheet and roast, stirring occasionally, until the peppers are very tender and jammy, 25 to 30 minutes. Let cool completely; transfer to a bowl and toss the peppers with the celery leaves.

3. Preheat the broiler. Spread the bread slices in an even layer on a baking sheet and toast them until golden, 1 to 2 minutes. Immediately rub each slice with garlic and drizzle with oil.

4. To serve, mound the peppers on top of the bread slices. Garnish each crostini with either a single anchovy fillet or capers (about ½ teaspoon per crostini), if desired.

Port-glazed Stilton with homemade oat biscuits

Port-glazed Stilton is the ultimate holiday cocktail party fare. It requires absolutely no real work but is highly impressive, elevating the usual cheese platter into something epicurean.

Usually I serve it with purchased oat crackers, the kind imported from England. But once, feeling tired of paying $5 for a teensy package, I decided to try making my own.

They were simpler than I imagined. You just mix the ingredients with your fingers until the dough comes together, then pat or roll it out and cut into squares. I've made them into thicker, heartier crackers and thinner, more delicate crackers and I prefer the thinner ones, though they'll crumble if you're too aggressive with the Stilton smearing.

And the cheese itself is beyond easy: You just boil down cheap ruby Port wine with sugar, bay leaf, and black pepper until it's syrupy, then drizzle the syrup over a wedge of the best Stilton you can procure. The syrup takes on a musky, spicy, herbal taste from the seasonings and adds a welcome touch of sweetness to the salty, rich cheese.

Of course, you can also serve the syrup-gilded cheese with purchased crackers or bread. With results this festive and attractive, no one could fault you for not going all out.

serves 8

½ cup sugar

½ cup ruby Port

½ teaspoon freshly ground black pepper

1 bay leaf

1 (1-pound) wedge Stilton cheese

Grapes, for serving

Oat Biscuits (recipe follows) or store-bought oat crackers or bread, for serving

1. In a large saucepan, combine the sugar, Port, pepper, and bay leaf and bring to a boil. Cook over moderate heat, stirring occasionally, until thickened enough to coat the back of a spoon, about 5 minutes. Discard the bay leaf and let cool. (The syrup can be made 1 week ahead and refrigerated; bring to room temperature before serving.)

2. To serve, set the Stilton on a serving platter and drizzle the Port syrup over the cheese. Serve with grapes and oat biscuits or other crackers and/or bread.

(continued)

Oat biscuits

makes 20 oat biscuits

1 cup whole wheat or all-purpose flour, plus more for dusting

1½ tablespoons sugar

½ teaspoon baking soda

½ teaspoon kosher salt, plus more for sprinkling

1½ cups old-fashioned rolled oats

½ cup (1 stick) unsalted butter

¼ cup plain full-fat yogurt

1. Preheat the oven to 350°F. Lightly grease a baking sheet or line it with parchment paper.

2. In a large bowl, mix together the flour, sugar, baking soda, and salt. Stir in the oats and, using your fingers, rub in the butter to form a coarse meal. Fold in the yogurt.

3. On a lightly floured surface, roll the dough into a rectangle ³⁄₁₆ inch thick. Cut the dough into 20 rectangles and transfer to the prepared baking sheet.

4. Sprinkle the oat biscuits with additional kosher salt, if desired, and bake for about 15 minutes, or until the edges are dark golden brown. Place the baking sheet on a wire rack and allow the oat biscuits to cool for 5 minutes, then transfer to the wire rack to finish cooling. Store in an airtight container.

Stupendous hummus

I'd never thought too hard about the divide between the pretty good hummus I'd throw together in the food processor and the extraordinary hummus I ate at certain Middle Eastern restaurants around town. My hummus was certainly tasty—garlic laden, lemony, and mixed with good, peppery olive oil and dashes of cumin and cayenne. It came together in minutes with a minimum of fuss, and for years that was good enough for me.

Then I made the mistake of trying out a hummus recipe from Mitchell Davis's wonderful book *Kitchen Sense*. He's a terrific cook who knows his stuff. So when he proclaimed a hummus recipe the best you've ever tasted, well, I had to try it.

There are two things that make Mitchell's recipe different from most: he insists upon using freshly cooked chickpeas instead of canned, he also strongly implores you to peel the peas.

Yup, you read that right. Peel the chickpeas—each, individual, tiny little pea.

I tried it and it was so time consuming I knew I'd ever do it again.

But cooking the peas from scratch? Now, *that* I could handle. I then pureed them with the usual cumin-garlic-tahini-lemon mixture.

Mitchell was right. With a rich, almost toasty flavor from the freshly cooked garbanzos that enhanced the fragrance of the spices, which I also sprinkled on top as a potent garnish, it really was by leaps and bounds the best hummus I'd ever made. And I didn't even have to peel the peas.

makes about 3½ cups

Freshly squeezed juice of 1 lemon, plus more for serving

1 teaspoon kosher salt

½ teaspoon ground cumin

½ teaspoon freshly ground black pepper

1 fat garlic clove or 2 smaller cloves, finely chopped

Pinch cayenne, plus more for serving

⅓ cup tahini

3 cups cooked chickpeas, preferably cooked up from dried peas (see Note)

½ cup extra-virgin olive oil, plus more for drizzling

Cumin Salt (see page 40) or flaky sea salt, for serving

1. Combine the lemon juice, kosher salt, cumin, black pepper, garlic, and cayenne in a food processor. Pulse the mixture a few times until the liquid whirls around just enough to blend together. Drop in the tahini and ½ cup water. Pulse until

(continued)

smooth. Add the chickpeas and puree until smooth and creamy. This might take several minutes, but stick with it. With the motor running, drizzle in the oil until the mixture is combined. Taste and adjust the flavors if you think it needs it; you might need to add a pinch of salt. I used 1¼ teaspoons, but it teetered on that edge of perfectly salted and too salty, so I cut it back in the ingredients list. If you do add salt, dissolve it first in a few drops of lemon juice or warm water.

2. Spread the hummus on a plate. Top it with a generous drizzle of olive oil, a squeeze of lemon juice, and a dash of cayenne. Finish with a sprinkling of cumin salt or sea salt, and serve.

note: To cook your own chickpeas, soak 1 cup of them overnight in a large bowl of cold, heavily salted water, drain, then simmer in a pot of (new) heavily salted water with 4 peeled garlic cloves until tender, usually about 1 hour. (Discard the garlic.) If you don't soak them overnight, they will take 2 to 3 hours to cook, depending on the age of the beans. A cup of dried chickpeas yields 3 cups cooked.

Cheater's pork and ginger dumplings

I was in college when my family starting making a habit of going for dim sum in Chinatown, a perfect halfway point between my parents in Flatbush and school. Since I certainly wasn't going to waste a weekend night having dinner with my parents, a weekend breakfast of dim sum seemed just right.

And thus the ritual began. My parents insisted that the freshest and best dim sum was to be had early in the morning, so we always met one Sunday a month around ten a.m., finishing before the legions descended.

Having dim sum became the time I spent with my family, and it remains a cornerstone to this day. It was at dim sum that I introduced my parents to my more serious boyfriends, putting them through what I called "trial by dim sum." Now I bring my husband and daughter, or a group of friends. With a crowd, we can sample a wide variety of little dishes as they pass on steel carts, pushed by uniformed women who announce their cargo in Cantonese as they go from table to table. Dishes come quickly in what seems like a never-ending succession: deep-fried crab balls, tripe, congee, green scallion dumplings, shrimp rice noodles, fried eggplant, snails in black bean sauce, mussels with chiles, and soft, slightly sweet pork buns—a favorite with friends who would rather be at brunch.

And if Canal Street on a weekend morning isn't in the cards, there is always the possibility of making cheaters' dumplings at home. It could be a ritual unto itself.

makes 24 dumplings

1 tablespoon soy sauce, plus more for dipping

1 teaspoon toasted (Asian) sesame oil

¼ pound shiitake mushrooms, stemmed and caps wiped clean

½ pound ground pork

1 large egg white

2 scallions, finely chopped

2 teaspoons cornstarch

1 teaspoon grated peeled fresh ginger

1 teaspoon mirin or sherry

Pinch kosher salt

Large pinch ground white pepper

24 (3-inch) round gyoza or wonton wrappers, or (4-inch) square wrappers, cut into 3-inch rounds

Bok choy, cabbage, or lettuce leaves, for lining the steamer (optional)

1. Preheat the broiler. Arrange an oven rack 6 inches from the heat source.

(continued)

2. In a bowl, whisk together the soy sauce and sesame oil. Place the mushroom caps on a baking sheet. Brush both sides lightly with the soy sauce mixture (reserve what's left for the pork mixture). Broil the mushrooms, turning once halfway through, until golden brown and almost dry to the touch, about 8 minutes. Let cool slightly; finely chop the mushrooms.

3. In a large bowl, combine the remaining soy mixture, mushrooms, pork, egg white, scallions, cornstarch, ginger, mirin or sherry, salt, and pepper; mix well.

4. Line a baking sheet with parchment paper. Place a gyoza or wonton wrapper on a clean work surface. Brush the tops of the wrappers lightly with water. Place a scant tablespoon of pork mixture in the center of the wrapper. Pinch the edges up around the filling, leaving the top open. Transfer the finished dumpling to the lined baking sheet; repeat with the remaining dumplings.

5. Fill a large pot with ½ inch water. Place a steamer basket inside the pot (it should just fit); line the basket with bok choy, cabbage, or lettuce leaves, if desired, to prevent sticking. Arrange the dumplings in a single layer inside the basket (cook the dumplings in batches if they do not all fit). Steam the dumplings, covered, over high heat, until the pork is cooked through, about 15 minutes. Transfer to a platter and serve, with additional soy sauce for dipping.

Crispy onion fritters with whole spices and hot sauce

Entrenched on the couch, bone tired after a long day, I groaned to my husband, Daniel, that there was nothing in the house to eat. Daniel knows to translate "there's nothing to eat" into "let's order in," despite the fully stocked fridge, freezer, and pantry.

While I was perusing the takeout menu of our favorite local Indian restaurant, I spotted the spiced onion fritters called pakoras and wished we could order them. At the restaurant, they are golden brown perfection, with a brittle crust containing a slew of slithery, cumin-scented onions. They don't work for takeout, though, turning limp and sad during the five-block trek.

We placed the order sans pakoras, but the image of those fritters stayed in my head, and nothing short of whipping up a batch would rid me of it. The only potential flaw in this plan was that all the pakora recipes I found online used chickpea flour as the base, probably the one thing I don't keep in my overstuffed cupboard. Regular flour and an egg (to make up for the binding qualities of the legume flour) would have to do.

We ate them while they were hot, squirted with Sriracha and lime juice, and they were meaty, sweet, and spicy without being so filling that they ruined our appetite for *chana saag* when it finally arrived.

And the best thing about onion fritters, I thought as I munched, is that even if, there really wasn't much in the house to eat, I'll always have all the ingredients on hand.

makes 24 fritters

½ teaspoon cumin seeds

½ teaspoon coriander seeds

1 cup all-purpose flour

1 teaspoon baking powder

½ teaspoon kosher salt, plus more for serving

1 cup whole milk or water

1 large egg

¼ teaspoon freshly squeezed lime juice (optional)

¼ teaspoon Tabasco sauce

1 large onion, sliced lengthwise (top to bottom) into ¼-inch-thick slices

Canola or vegetable oil, for frying

Lime wedges, for serving (optional)

Hot sauce, such as Sriracha or harissa, for serving (optional)

(continued)

1. With a mortar and pestle, lightly crush the cumin and coriander seeds (the aim is to break them up, not to grind them to a powder; you want texture and crunch). In a large bowl, whisk together the flour, baking powder, salt, and spices. In a separate bowl, whisk together the milk, egg, lime juice (if using), and Tabasco.

2. Whisk the flour mixture into the milk mixture until just blended (do not overmix). The batter should be slightly thicker in texture than cream; if it's too thick, thin with a little bit of milk, or if it's too thin, sprinkle with additional flour. Stir in the onions. Let the mixture rest for 10 to 30 minutes.

3. Meanwhile, fill a large pot halfway with oil and heat until the temperature registers 375°F on a deep-fry thermometer.

4. Working in batches, drop the battered onions by the tablespoon into the oil. Fry, turning occasionally, until golden all over, 2 to 3 minutes total. Use a slotted spoon to transfer the onions to a paper towel–lined plate to drain. Sprinkle with salt and serve, with lime wedges and hot sauce, if desired.

Cornmeal blini with salmon caviar

Every holiday season, I always find an excuse to make these luxurious cornmeal blinis with crème fraîche and caviar. Whether I'm having a full-fledged holiday party, or a small Christmas Eve dinner for a few friends, I'll fry up a batch of the tiny, buttery, grainy pancakes; top them with crème fraîche and the best caviar I can afford in a given year; and serve them with Champagne. If caviar isn't your bag (or your budget), fortunately the world is full of delicious blini-topping alternatives: smoked salmon, fresh ricotta and honey, crumbled blue cheese and chives, or Greek yogurt and pomegranate seeds.

Whatever your preference, I don't think there's anything more festive to kick off a celebratory meal.

makes 36 blinis

1 cup fine cornmeal

1 cup all-purpose flour

½ teaspoon baking soda

1 teaspoon baking powder

1 teaspoon kosher salt

1 tablespoon sugar

3 large eggs, lightly beaten

1 cup buttermilk or plain yogurt

1 cup milk

4 tablespoons (½ stick) unsalted butter, melted

Olive oil, for frying

2 cups crème fraîche

Salmon roe or other caviar, for topping

Snipped fresh chives, for topping

1. Preheat the oven to 250°F.

2. In a medium bowl, combine the cornmeal, flour, baking soda, baking powder, salt, and sugar and stir well to mix. Add the eggs, buttermilk or yogurt, milk, and melted butter and mix until smooth.

3. Heat a skillet over medium heat until hot, then brush with oil. Using a spoon and working in small batches, drop tablespoons of batter into the pan. When bubbles form evenly on the top of the blini, turn (just once) and cook until golden.

4. Transfer the first batch of cooked blini to a heatproof plate lined with paper towels and keep warm, covered, in the oven. Repeat with the remaining batter.

5. To serve, top each warm blini with a dollop of crème fraîche, a smaller dollop of salmon caviar, and a sprinkling of chives. Serve immediately.

index

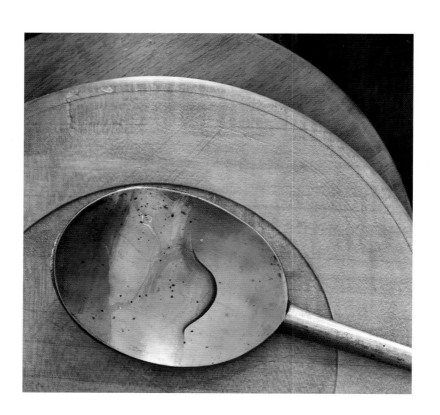